The Analog Sea Review

NUMBER ONE

THE ANALOG SEA REVIEW · NUMBER ONE

Copyright © 2018, 2022 Analog Sea

Second Edition, 2022

"The London Library" by E.M. Forster
from *Two Cheers for Democracy*
Copyright © 1939 by E.M. Forster
Reprinted by permission of HMH Trade Publishing

"Vita Contemplativa" by Byung-Chul Han
from *Scent of Time*
Copyright © 1992 by Polity Press
Reprinted by permission of Polity Books

"When Death Comes" by Mary Oliver
from *New and Selected Poems*
Copyright © 1992 by Mary Oliver
Reprinted by permission of
The Charlotte Sheedy Literary Agency Inc.

Printed in Germany

Published by Analog Sea
PO Box 11670
Austin, Texas 78711
United States

Editors Jonathan S. Simons,
Janos Tedeschi, and Elena Fritz

Cover Artwork
Joseph-Antoine d'Ornano

ISBN 978-1-7322519-0-8

The Analog Sea Review
Number One

FROM THE EDITOR *Jonathan Simons* — I

THEY WOULD ALWAYS TOUCH THE EARTH *Trebbe Johnson* — 3

THE PERSISTENCE OF MEMORY *Carl Sagan* — 6

THE HEADLAND *Matthew Hollis* — 7

INTERVIEW WITH PATRICK SHEN *Analog Sea Editors* — 8

SELF-RELIANCE *Ralph Waldo Emerson* — 21

CONJECTURES OF A GUILTY BYSTANDER *Thomas Merton* — 22

FORM OUT OF FORMLESSNESS *Patrick Shen* — 23

DEVOTIONAL CINEMA *Nathaniel Dorsky* — 26

THE AUDIBLE BREATH *Urs Hafner* — 27

LETTER TO THE EDITOR *Dan G.* — 30

WRITER'S PARADISE *Matthew Feeney* — 34

AFFLUENCE WITHOUT ABUNDANCE *James Suzman* — 35

ANCIENT FOREST *Scott T. Starbuck* — 47

LETTER TO THE EDITOR *Dr. Patrick L.* — 48

INTERVIEW WITH JOSEPH-ANTOINE D'ORNANO *Kyra Levine* — 49

THERE IS A VITALITY *Martha Graham* — 61

THE LONDON LIBRARY *E. M. Forster* — 62

LUNCH *Steven Doloff* — 68

VITA CONTEMPLATIVA *Byung-Chul Han* — 69

THE LIGHT IS DIFFERENT THERE *Lesley Saunders*   84

ONE BRIGHT DAY *Katharine Teleki*   90

INTERVIEW WITH GODFREY REGGIO *Richard Whittaker*   94

A SUNSET AND A CONE *William Oxley*   100

METAPHORA *Robert Ensor*   101

MUSIC, A LIFE-CHANGING FORCE *Jameela Siddiqi*   102

PROGRAM NOTES *Ravi Shankar In Concert*   111

INTERVIEW WITH JAMEELA SIDDIQI *Analog Sea Editors*   113

THE OLD POETS *Jonathan Simons*   125

LONELINESS AND HISTORY *Leonard Cohen*   126

SUNFLOWERS *Richard Ormrod*   133

I NEVER WANTED FAME *Antonio Machado*   135

WHEN DEATH COMES *Mary Oliver*   136

ARTWORK CREDITS   138

CONTRIBUTORS   139

From the Editor
Jonathan Simons

We find ourselves in a historical moment of pervasive mediocrity. Fueled by basic human drives—flights from death and boredom—the new technologies, bright and all-consuming, increasingly blur the lines between direct experience and representation. A photograph of an apple is not food and the Internet has neither scent nor texture.

Shifting our focus from representation back to direct experience is simple, at least once we remember the value in doing so. But like harvesting wild mushrooms, the differences between toxicity and sustenance can be subtle. Knowledge is needed, a shared knowledge refined through discussion, deepened through study, strengthened through discipline, and explored creatively. And when *depth experience* emerges and wipes the sleep from our eyes, we turn our gaze away from spectacle and back toward raw, unmediated life.

We call these ideas "the emerging field of offline culture" and seek out poems, essays, and artworks made by others who maintain deep connection with the natural world. But to illuminate the differences between direct experience and representation we need not only critical thought but also those vital faculties too easily atrophied by overstimulation—feeling, intuition, and imagination. When the bright lights of modernity burn into our eyes, we must remember that sustained attention can be honed. The strength to dream comes not only from intention but from practice.

With great appreciation for all of you now discovering the shores of Analog Sea, we present the inaugural edition of *The Analog Sea Review*.

They Would Always Touch the Earth
Trebbe Johnson

More than twenty years after the famous photo of Earthrise captivated people around the world, another image of the home planet showed up to make a different but no less emotional impact on a small group of scientists. That the photograph even existed was due to the persistent urging of the popular astronomer Carl Sagan. For more than ten years the Voyager spacecraft had been streaming farther and farther toward the outer reaches of the solar system, dutifully taking pictures of Jupiter and Saturn and sending them back to the Jet Propulsion Laboratory in Houston. Sagan noticed that there would come a brief point in Voyager's journey when the capsule would be in direct alignment with Earth, four billion miles away, and he began lobbying for a photo op. He wanted NASA officials to turn the spacecraft around just long enough so it could aim its camera at its planet of origin.

Implementing such a plan would take an additional six months and cost millions of dollars. Still, Sagan insisted: this was a rare opportunity the agency would be foolish to pass over. At last he prevailed. So the little orbiter was programmed to pivot around and take a picture of Earth.

The resulting image had none of the majesty of Earthrise. Instead of an orb of ocean and cloud suspended in lustrous black space, this photo showed pixilated bands of black, brown, mauve, and gray. Only some careful scrutiny revealed a tiny pale blue dot in the vast monotones of the cosmos. This little speck was Earth. The JPL employees who had been displaying photos of Voyager's journey added this one to the collection. But then something strange began to happen. The photo showing the pale blue dot had to be replaced again and again, because it kept getting smudged. For the longest time, no one could figure out why. Finally, according to Candace Hansen-Koharcheck, who worked at JPL at the time, they realized what was happening: "People would come up to look at it and they would always touch the Earth."[1]

They would always touch the Earth. The scientists saw that pale blue micro-dot, recognized it, and had to touch it. At that moment they were responding only partly as scientists and technicians; they were also responding as women and men caught up in amazement at the very presence of their distinctive home in the midst of so much that was patently not distinctive. There amidst the anonymous strands of the universe rolled our own Earth—unlikely, lovely, and no larger than a peppercorn—and they were filled with wonder. This drive for intimacy with the planet of our birth begins in infancy and never leaves us; we just develop the habit, as we grow older, of ignoring it. In order to retain our sanity in challenging times

---

1 Nell Greenfieldboyce, "An Alien View of Earth," *Weekend Edition*, National Public Radio (February 13, 2010).

and do our part in keeping the planet healthy, it is essential that we relearn the knack of touching the Earth.

From Trebbe Johnson, *Radical Joy for Hard Times: Finding Meaning and Making Beauty in Earth's Broken Places* (Berkeley, California: North Atlantic Books, 2018).

The Persistence of Memory
Carl Sagan

What an astonishing thing a book is. It's a flat object made from a tree with flexible parts on which are imprinted lots of funny dark squiggles. But one glance at it and you're inside the mind of another person, maybe somebody dead for thousands of years. Across the millennia, an author is speaking clearly and silently inside your head, directly to you. Writing is perhaps the greatest of human inventions, binding together people who never knew each other, citizens of distant epochs. Books break the shackles of time. A book is proof that humans are capable of working magic.

From *Cosmos*, episode 11, "The Persistence of Memory," directed by Adrian Malone, written by Carl Sagan, aired December 7, 1980, on PBS.

The Headland
Matthew Hollis

Coast in its cave like a walled bear,
not caring to be quartered or subdued,
though it bides for a floodtide or slips
into strata or reforms into air
it cannot die, being there at the dawn,
being half of me. If only I could climb down
from the headland, down between the needle
and the shore, I might again claim time.
But dusk comes, and I have places of my own,
and I did not think to stay long, just longer,
with those who share in whatever may be:
the half in us that ages, the half that finds eternity.

Interview with Patrick Shen
Analog Sea Editors

W e live in a world of noise. From the seemingly inescapable automation and digitization of everyday objects to the unbridled growth of urban centers, from the screens blaring in public spaces to the decibel levels of the human voices around us — the volume seems to be rising with each passing day. The search for stillness, for a quiet space of one's own — a space where one can think, grow, create, or simply be — seems increasingly difficult. How to rectify the need for silence and solitude with the cacophony of modern life?

Award-winning director of documentary films Patrick Shen has spent decades examining the human experience. His critically acclaimed film, *In Pursuit of Silence*, is an immersive cinematic journey around the globe that invites the viewer to experience silence.

The Analog Sea Review editors Jonathan Simons and Janos Tedeschi sat down recently with Patrick to discuss his work ahead of a special screening of *In Pursuit of Silence* at *The Analog Sea Review* journal launch in Zurich.

ANALOG SEA: In her essay "The Aesthetics of Silence," Susan Sontag writes, "So far as he is serious, the artist is continually tempted to sever the dialog he has with an audience. Silence is the furthest extension of that reluctance to communicate, that ambivalence about making contact with the audience which is a leading motif of modern art. ... Silence is the artist's ultimate otherworldly gesture: by silence, he frees himself from servile bondage to the world, which appears as patron, client, consumer, antagonist, arbiter, and distorter of his work."[1]

It seems to us that the more we work with these topics of solitude and silence, or Ernest Becker's writing, for example, the more they work on us. And then, for better or worse, a deconstruction process ensues and we're back to that Emersonian puzzle of being in the world but not of it. One goes into the world to spark connections and find meaning but then often gets burned. A longing to retreat from the world emerges—a longing for silence. For example, the work we're doing now with Analog Sea is so utterly worldly, so deeply engaged with commerce and ego. We think a lot about solitude and silence, as well as gift-giving and how to make the world a little more beautiful. But navigating this razor's edge between solitude and social engagement is an interesting challenge. Does your work making films motivate you to be in the world, to retreat from it, or do you experience a similar cycle?

PATRICK SHEN: It does feel like a cycle of retreating from the world and then returning to it for a while, which is what

---

[1]   Susan Sontag, "The Aesthetics of Silence," in *Studies of Radical Will* (New York: Farrar, Straus and Giroux, 1969).

I've been doing for three years now with this film [*In Pursuit of Silence*].

Thomas Merton said something once about how when you introduce too many projects and too many people into your life it has a violent effect on the nature of the work you're doing and the nature of your spirit at that moment. In a sense, it's an existential battle. I do think it's important that we continue offering bits and pieces of our consciousness and spirit so as to contribute to the collective narrative. The world needs people who retreat from the world in order to see it more clearly. Then we can create these expressions of our consciousness and give them back as offerings. I think it's important that we take part in that activity. It's kind of what sustains humanity—the people who feel that it's important to protect those creative spaces, those places of silence and stillness, and then offer bits and pieces of it to others. Even if only one or two people ultimately receive the offering, it's important for it to exist.

At the same time, it's also important that we don't isolate ourselves completely from the world lest we become quite self-important and inaccessible. It's something that I struggle with, for sure. I haven't quite figured out how to wrap my brain around it but it seems we do need to become part of the world, at least for certain periods of time, before we retreat from it, so that we don't end up risking irrelevance and inaccessibility.

AS: I hope it's clear that we are not romanticizing solitude. It's in those places that we must reconcile deeper and darker parts of ourselves, and that can be quite painful. This makes me think about your new film on shadows. Although we have no idea yet how you might translate this broad topic of shadows into a film, can you share with us some of what shadow means to you?

PS: In literature, shadow tends to mean the darker side of human nature. But it represents more than that to me. It represents the authentic nature of our being, the side that can exist in the world without the need to be seen by the world. Our cultural selves are quite the opposite. We wear these many layers of armor in order to navigate society and yet those layers often feel unreal, don't they? Shadows, on the other hand, are daily reminders of who we really are. How great would it be at the end of watching the film, for better or worse, to have people start paying a little bit more attention to their own shadow — that version of themselves that can exist in the world but without the need to be seen or measured against what everyone else is doing?

AS: You mention "attention," which is a crucial word for us at Analog Sea. Faculties of attention are the keys to experience, don't you think? To what extent might one notice, walking through a bank lobby or even a friend's living room, that they are walking on an incredibly elaborate Persian carpet? To what extent does one notice nature around them, the migration of birds, the shifting of seasons? Do you think much about this topic and have your films taught you to pay more attention to the world around you?

PS: Ultimately, I feel this is what we're all after. Whether it's your work with Analog Sea or the films I make, we are honing a hyperawareness of who we are and where we are at any given moment. That's precisely what the online world pulls us away from. Not that technology is inherently bad, but that's what it does; it removes us from the natural space where we actually are to the point where we really don't need to pay attention because everything comes to us. We don't need to find whatever it is we are looking for, because it finds us.

In part, my films have been my own way of forcing myself to pay attention to something for an extended period of time, like in meditation. I'm exploring my curiosity so as to create an offering through that curiosity but I'm also doing it for my own benefit, for my own personal growth. Making a film is a deep dive. It's like going to school for three or four years. You come out at the end of it a completely different person, for sure. I'm grateful to have a job where I can explore something deeply that I happen to be curious about and to come out the other end a little bit better than I was before. So, do I think about attention? All the time, man. All the time. I'm desperate to have that capacity back like we had as children. I'm desperate to regain that capacity to pay attention. I feel like I'm being pulled away all the time. We all are. And it grates on my soul, you know?

What do you guys think about attention? How do you maintain a sense of attention throughout your days?

AS: The question we struggle with are the conditions most conducive to paying attention and being fully present. If I have a smartphone that constantly sends me notifications, I'm repeatedly being pulled away from the moment and my environment. I understand that I must engage with technology and find a balanced way of using e-mail and the Internet, perhaps giving it a dedicated space in my life so as not to be perpetually connected. But that's just one condition. Another is how I socialize with people and what kind of friendships I choose to nurture. There's this beautiful stanza in Rilke's *The Book of Hours*, in which he writes, "I want, in the hushed moments when the nameless draws near, to be among the wise ones—or alone."[2] That really speaks to us.

Something we also talk a lot about is this dialectic between primary depth experience and secondary representation.

---

2 Rainer Maria Rilke, "The Book of a Monastic Life," in *Rilke's Books of Hours: Love Poems to God*, trans. Anita Barrow and Joanna Macy (New York: Riverhead Books, 2005), p. 67. Book first published in German as *Das Stunden-Buch* in 1905.

One of our concerns about the world we're now living in is that with all the information coming at us, most of which is fragmented from the start, a lot of people will go a very long time, if not forever, without depth experience and the power it has to realign one's life in positive ways.

PS: It's true, so much of what we consume now is secondary experience. It's the Instagram feed, for example, and how we're constantly engaging with other people's secondary experience to the extent that we begin to see ourselves and the world through this lens. The world now is like a dangerous trick because while we are flooded with secondary representation what we all really want—even if we don't always know it so clearly—is for depth experience to be our primary way of experiencing our world. But we seem to lack the tools and strategies to flip the narrative.

AS: Would you say that your film about silence speaks of stillness as one of these strategies? Are silence and stillness pathways to a deeper way of experiencing life?

PS: Silence is one way to understand and talk about it. It's a mode of being in which we're porous to the world. When we're amid noise, whether internal or external, we're closed off. We shut down parts of our being in order to navigate the moments when there's too much going on and too much coming in. Whereas when it's quiet, again whether internally or externally, we thrive; the pores of our being open up, the world permeates through us, and we're able to truly connect with the space around us or the person sitting across from us. So I absolutely think silence is a doorway to depth experience.

AS: So where is all of this heading? Where are the poets and the philosophers and filmmakers going to emerge from in the coming years?

PS: We're in great need of poets and philosophers and filmmakers. As George Prochnik—the author of the book, *In Pursuit of Silence,*[3] from which I borrowed the title—said, it was noise that won our most recent presidential election. That's the mode that we're in as a nation. Noise is the new default. It's the loudest person in the room that is heard. All the research proves that is utter nonsense, that the ideas of the quiet person in the room are just as good as anyone else's. We need to counteract that narrative but I don't know how. I know that we need to keep contributing our ideas but we should also avoid becoming part of the problem itself. We can't just respond to the noise. We have to respond from a more meaningful space, from a frame of mind somehow connected to stillness and silence. Because any direct response

---

3 George Prochnik, *In Pursuit of Silence* (New York: Doubleday, 2010).

to noise is just more noise. Whether or not people will listen is a whole other matter and I don't know what to do about that. It saddens me when I think about the fact that I spend all of this time and energy trying to make a pure piece of creative work only to find that very few people actually appreciate and watch it. It's not easy, this work of changing hearts and shifting perspectives.

AS: For those of us who think and feel deeply, and find it valuable to maintain sustained attention, how do we create a platform in order to find other artists who are doing the same? Do we go online? Do we create Facebook pages for Analog Sea and your films? In other words, how do we find other like-minded artists and thinkers without reverting to platforms that are inherently fragmented?

PS: People want real experiences because they are starting to feel that these secondary virtual experiences are not as meaningful. They fade very quickly. So I think we crave something more substantial and authentic. So maybe there's something about these alternative models such as what Nathaniel Dorsky employs, projecting his films only in theaters on full-size screens, or what you're doing with the Analog Sea Offline Ball and other events supporting offline publishers and bookstores. I think there's an audience for it. For me, it's counterintuitive to introduce these initiatives on the Internet and to make them a virtual thing even if those digital platforms might expand the outreach of these endeavors. It's important that you guys maintain your offline model. Do you struggle with that? Are you drawn to the idea of starting a Facebook group to expand your membership?

AS: While we are certainly not against the Internet and use it almost daily, we've discovered that there are definitely people out there who are inspired by something existing these days only in the physical world. And on a visceral level, we just don't want to participate in the madness the Internet has become. It's a relief to send off more paper letters than e-mails. We believe that the Internet is a helpful tool but not a new planet we want to immigrate to full time.

If you think about it, human beings have always wanted to replace reality with a more controllable, disembodied, and therefore less painful, replica. The Athenians had their epic tragedies which effectively intoxicated the masses for days on end. Much later, the invention of the radio brought an unceasing stream of noise into the home. And then television arrived with its soap operas and so-called reality programming.

This mad dream of humanity is just now coming into fruition and that is an uninterrupted virtual world that seems to sustain our basic needs, but which we ultimately control. We upload pictures of what we eat, we meet our friends and family, we explore sex and dating, read the news, entertain ourselves ceaselessly, all online. What's excluded? Only the body is excluded. But it's precisely the body we want most to exclude from our virtual reality because it's the body which faces old age, sickness, and eventually death. So long as grid power flows and the batteries remain charged, the virtual world provides us with a believable substitute to human experience but without the discomfort of a lonely and hungry body hanging out in a silent room. But how does a human being actually develop—whether we're speaking in terms of empathy or the longing to create a work of art—now that we've essentially eradicated boredom?

PS: That's exactly it. The writer Pico Iyer, who we feature in the film, talks about how our lives are now like a canvas we're standing only an inch away from. We have no sense of the big picture and are forgetting what it's like to be a whole person navigating these spaces. We're not taking time to collect our thoughts on who we are and what the best version of ourselves might be. We're just occupying space and maintaining and sustaining the current narratives. We're tranquilized by all the distraction and stimulation. We're doing all the work that makes the world go around and continue as it has been. But what about the work that's required to make it move forward? That is done on the fringes, isn't it? The mainstream has always been distracted by the latest and greatest trends. It's those on the fringes who have taken time to leave the context of the world so as to have the time and space to think. In the end, it's just as simple as taking time to think and reflect on what's going on.

AS: Even the fringes seem now completely absorbed by the Internet. Wasn't it always the poets and artists who sought depth experience? Now many of them venture with great passion into this brave new virtual world we're co-creating. I've met artists who study fine arts but have never created anything in pencil or watercolor. They work exclusively on their phones and tablets and the conservatoires seem to promote it.

PS: Perhaps it's partly the excitement of finding an audience online. Many artists go through—as John Cage would say—this school of self-importance. Cage rejected the idea of work altogether. The idea of the genius artists, he rejected all of that. Because the second you consider who you are making it for is the moment the work starts losing meaning. I think there's a lot of wisdom in that. The Internet is so attractive to those seeking an audience. It cuts out the gatekeepers, the middleman; you can have direct engagement with your audience, you can make money, you can be seen and heard and therefore maintain your narrative of self-importance. Considering how addictive it is, this constant feedback from the crowd, it's no surprise that it's consuming all of us.

And then there's the monastic model. There are people who retreat from the world, not necessarily fleeing from it, sometimes staying within urban monasteries. Theirs is often a longing to gain perspective about the human condition, a path that inevitably leads them to contemplate not only their own lives but also the despair and corruption they previously observed in society. What they developed was a lifestyle of contemplation. I think this is an interesting model for how we can move forward as artists and poets, so as to continue creating work in difficult times. The act of retreating from the world, and creating from that sense of spaciousness can certainly be a productive response to what's happening in the world. Once the individual gets a taste of this experience of retreat, what we're calling depth experience, he or she will want more. It changes everything. That introduction is ultimately what I believe we, as artists, are trying to achieve.

In addition to making films, Patrick Shen lectures and teaches filmmaking workshops all over the globe as a film envoy for the U.S. State Department and the USC School of Cinematic Arts American Film Showcase. He recently co-authored a book entitled *Notes on Silence* and is currently at work on a new slate of films which include two experimental works, *In Praise of Shadows* and *Four Minutes*.

Self-Reliance
Ralph Waldo Emerson

I t is easy in the world to live after the world's opinion; it is easy in solitude to live after our own; but the great man is he who in the midst of the crowd keeps with perfect sweetness the independence of solitude.

From Ralph Waldo Emerson, "Self-Reliance," in *The Complete Essays and Other Writings of Ralph Waldo Emerson* (New York: Random House, 1950), p. 150. Essay first published in *Essays: First Series* in 1841.

Conjectures of a Guilty Bystander
Thomas Merton

There is a pervasive form of contemporary violence to which the idealist most easily succumbs: activism and overwork. The rush and pressure of modern life are a form, perhaps the most common form, of its innate violence. To allow oneself to be carried away by a multitude of conflicting concerns, to surrender to too many demands, to commit oneself to too many projects, to want to help everyone in everything, is to succumb to violence. The frenzy of our activism neutralizes our work for peace. It destroys our own inner capacity for peace. It destroys the fruitfulness of our own work, because it kills the root of inner wisdom which makes work fruitful.

From Thomas Merton, *Conjectures of a Guilty Bystander* (New York: Doubleday, 1966), p. 73.

Form Out of Formlessness
Patrick Shen

I lost count of how many times someone suggested we change the title of my new film *In Pursuit of Silence* to something more scientifically honest—for example, *In Pursuit of Quiet*. I'm grateful to these early critics for forcing us to define the scope of the film and grapple with the inherent paradoxes and challenges we were up against. How can one portray silence *visually* and what does a film soundtrack exploring silence even sound like? These are questions we grappled with continuously throughout the three-year process.

I considered making a silent film, one resembling perhaps the work of one of my cinematic heroes, Nathaniel Dorsky, whose entire body of work is silent. But that would have required a level of maturity I felt I hadn't yet achieved.

I also found the conventional documentary format problematic and, well, noisy. Silence, after all, exists in the space between our words and points to a reality beyond them. Wouldn't any attempt to discuss silence simply shatter the very material I intended to pay homage to?

As the Japanese might suggest, the qualities of the silence we encounter are defined by our surroundings, past experiences, memories, and even our emotional state. The hushed voices of a museum experienced after a bustling city sidewalk have vastly different qualities than the dead quiet of an empty church interrupted by the sporadic creak of a wooden pew.

One person feels a sense of nostalgia in an old church whereas another finds it suffocating. One person's journey into silence doesn't and shouldn't resemble the next person's.

"Not only does silence exist in a world full of speech and other sounds, but any given silence takes its identity as a stretch of time being perforated by sound." —Susan Sontag [1]

And so I began to ponder my own journey with silence for some clues. I thought about the existential yearnings of adolescence that sparked my journey inward as well as a particular newspaper listing that led to me a movie theater one afternoon in 2007 to see *Into Great Silence*,[2] the beautiful film by Philip Gröning. I read again the words of authors and poets like Max Picard, Nathaniel Dorsky, Mary Oliver, Rilke, Rumi, Henry David Thoreau, John Cage and Pico Iyer, and others who write in ways that embody silence rather than merely attempt to demystify it. Then there was the music of composers like John Cage, Goldmund, and Arvo Pärt who seem to see silence as a collaborator rather than a space with which to fill ego.

My journey with silence had been informed by many experiences of words, both spoken and written, of sounds,

---

1 Susan Sontag, "The Aesthetics of Silence," in *Studies of Radical Will* (New York: Farrar, Straus and Giroux, 1969).

2 *Into Great Silence*, directed by Philip Gröning (New York: Zeitgeist Films, 2005), HDCAM, 162 minutes. Filmed in France, Switzerland, and Germany.

and images as well. These experiences gave me the freedom to explore the spaces between and I began to discover how inextricably tied silence and speech really are.

These insights inspired those of us making the film to explore silence in a manner that mimicked our direct experiences. Just as the world informed my journey into silence thus far, so could the film provide insight, context, and most importantly, freedom to explore the spaces between. So we began the work of filmmaking and the delicate process of selecting metaphors that we hoped would most honestly portray silence. A portrait that would—as all portraits do—capture a glimpse of something much larger and more complex, reflections as they appear to an artist in a particular context and at a specific moment of time.

There are no definitive answers as to what a film exploring silence should look or sound like. However, it is clear that we must think of silence not as a vacuum or as nothingness but as a much more complex phenomenon that includes the experience of being human in the world.

"How strange this silence would seem without these crickets here to explain." —William Michaelian [3]

---

3 William Michaelian, *Akitsu Quarterly* (Summer, 2015).

Devotional Cinema
Nathaniel Dorsky

I f we do relinquish control, we suddenly see a hidden world, one that has existed all along right in front of us. In a flash, the uncanny presence of the poetic and vibrant world, ripe with mystery, stands before us.

From Nathaniel Dorsky, *Devotional Cinema* (Berkeley, California: Tuumba Press, 2005), p. 37.

The Audible Breath
Urs Hafner

While still on the phone, people hurry along the streets, yammering about with a little device on their ear, saying over and over *Do you hear me? Are you still there? I'll call you back in a minute*. One spends half the conversation making sure this seemingly advanced device is simply serving its purpose.

The corded telephone set had a sluggish dial that was time-consuming and even cumbersome to operate. Yet it was precisely these moments that increased the anticipation (and sometimes fear) of the ensuing encounter. Even the solitary action of dialing granted some element of closeness: one felt the noticeable presence of the other even while he was absent.

Forces of Attraction

THE PHILOSOPHER THEODOR W. ADORNO (that sensitive, paternalistic charmer) wrote in the *Minima Moralia* that every woman, while speaking into the telephone, somehow sounds pretty: "The sound reflects certainty, implicitness, self-identity; a harkening back to all the glances of admiration and desire she has ever felt." Moreover, he concluded that since "seeing" beauty was not limited to the visual sense, it was easier to immediately recognize when on the phone: it is the "intimate citation of the never seen."

People found each other appealing on the phone, not only because they longed for the other due to physical absence. Using the phone made open, lighthearted chatter possible because the listener's appraising and perhaps bewitching eyes were not there to distract. Attraction blossomed, not least because physical absence opened the space for daydreams of desire. All this required sitting still and imagining—thanks to the stationary activity of conversing on a phone that didn't move around.

The immobility of the device demanded the user's patient presence. He could not go away, not digress, not wash dishes. He sat in the chair, he listened, he continued talking. Maybe the person on the other end solved a crossword puzzle or dozed off, but she was there—there, in front of her device.

Insensitive Technology

THE SOUND, MORE THAN ANYTHING, was different. The sound quality was so good that you could hear even the finest nuances of voice: every tremor of excitement, even a soft laugh. When one person was silent, the other heard him breathe and swallow; you even registered your own sigh. The digital transmission of the mobile phone, on the other hand, transmits only clear tones, which are reproduced in a "converted" and sometimes minimally time-delayed manner (or so the layman imagines), turning the hesitation, pausing, and silence into nothing but dead silence. This silence always raises the anxious question of whether your interlocutor can hear you, or is even still there.

Mobile phoning dredges up early childhood feelings of loneliness. When you remain silent, it cuts you off from the other person and separates you from them; this interrupts the conversation and destroys the connection. The mobile phone acts as a ruthless clock, dictating the breathless continuation of the dialogue. Silence is forbidden.

In allowing the quotidian sounds of swallowing and stammering, in clearing one's throat and sighing, in breathing and silence, the corded phone granted a certain togetherness. The unseen other was not only more beautiful: she was also closer, even in silent farewell, because if neither wanted to hang up the phone first, it was because they knew it could be for the last time.

From Urs Hafner, "Der hörbare Atem. Ein Nachruf auf das Kabeltelefon," *Neue Zürcher Zeitung* (July 4, 2017). Translated by Analog Sea editors.

Letter to the Editor
Dan G.

Howdy and greetings from the bowels of the maximum security division of the federal prison system,
perhaps one of the most "offline" places in the so-called
"civilized world." I'm quite interested in your publication
and whole-heartedly enjoy the idea behind it. That being said,
I'd love to be put on the mailing list for your newsletter and
am not above begging and pleading for a back issue or sample
copy of the publication itself.

Not that you asked, but a little about myself and my
circumstances. I'm down to the last twelve months or so of
an eighty-four-month sentence for unarmed bank robbery.
Having worked like a dog since I was twelve years old, I
became fairly successful and by the age of twenty-five, I had a
home, a wife, and most everything I'd ever wanted out of life.
At the age of twenty-eight, my drug and alcohol addictions
got the better of me and I threw it all away. The last decade
has been a blur of suicide attempts, criminal convictions, and
a general disdain for myself.

Not long after I got locked up this last time, I found
out I was a writer. I also found out that trying to become
a published writer in prison is an arduous journey. Most of
the hurdles stem from the fact that this is such an "offline"
environment. My first inclination was to type this as a submission for your publication, but the items I need to purchase

to type my stories and poems would cost upwards of thirty dollars and with no outside support and an hourly wage of twelve cents for the GED tutoring that I do in here I can't counter that type of purchase! Not an offline hurdle, but a hurdle nonetheless.

Not having the ability to access the Internet makes me much more reliant upon myself; it makes my writing more personal. There's no thesaurus at a glance to help me find the right word to complete a couplet or cinch up a stanza. No Wikipedia or any other devices for fact checking or making me second guess myself. As a result, my writing is strictly me, for better or worse.

Truth be told, there's something exquisitely pure about sightseeing through some of the darkest, most desolate neighborhoods of my mind without an Alexa or Google or other information portal allowing me to distract or edit myself in favor of any current worldview or trend. Prison is at once the best and worst of writer's retreats. Walls to enclose you with nothing but time and your thoughts. Just some paper, a pencil, and this literary penitent.

Since I never did much writing when I was on "The Outside," I'm not sure what the ability to go online will do for my composition methods. I've grown quite fond of my minimalist technique (pen, paper, cup of coffee). The only plus I see in going online with my poetry and prose is for submissions. It seems that more and more venues are going to an online-only submission format.

Several months ago, I came into some money and was able to type up most of my body of work—several dozen poems and half as many short stories. I embarked on a submission binge and did quite well. It always amazed me how many times I would receive a letter back encouraging me to use the online submission system for whatever journal it was. I go pretty far out of my way to explain where I'm writing from, yet some people must still hold to the myth of "Club Fed" when it comes to the Bureau of Prisons! I can't hardly ever get a hot meal, let alone have access to a computer.

Luckily though, for every clueless literary vehicle hell-bent on electronic submissions, there seem to be a few editors and organizations who, if not value, at least seem to tolerate those of us who still do all of our literary undertakings the old-fashioned way. The offline way. That's why I'm interested in your publication.

Upon my release I will have completed a four-thousand-hour, US Department of Labor-sanctioned teacher's aide apprenticeship. Not sure if there's much opportunity for an ex-con educator out there, but I do enjoy teaching. Unfortunately, the fact that I will be homeless with virtually no support system, puts the odds of me either ending up dead or on my way back to prison within six months of my release through the roof.

Sorry for talking (writing) your ear off, but thank you so much for your time.

Respectfully,
Dan G.

United States Penitentiary, Canaan
Waymart, Pennsylvania

Writer's Paradise
Matthew Feeney

Author Augusten Burroughs said
"The secret to being a writer is that
You have to write.
It's not enough to think about writing
or to study literature
or plan a future life as an author.
You have to
lock yourself away,
alone,
and get to work."

Prison is a Writer's Paradise.
We just don't have the
Key
to our lock.

Affluence without Abundance
James Suzman

T his Canaan is no promised land. But understanding the long history of its impoverished Ju/'hoan Bushman residents may help us to map a path to the economic promised land, in which no one need work more than the fifteen-hour workweek that John Maynard Keynes famously predicted would be realized within our lifetimes.

Canaan is a sprawling squatter settlement on the outskirts of Gobabis, a small town that services Namibia's vast Kalahari cattle ranches. It is now home to around four thousand people. More than half of them are Ju/'hoansi, the most famous of the Kalahari's hunting and gathering "Bushmen" peoples.

I began working in the Kalahari in 1991. Since then I have lived and worked among almost all of southern Africa's San "Bushmen" peoples, from the war-ravaged !Kung and Kxoe as they dodged bullets during the last brutal phases of the Angolan civil war to the G/wikhoe forcibly removed from Botswana's vast Central Kalahari Game Reserve in 1997.

But it is only in Canaan that I have ever felt any sense of real helplessness. And this is not just because whenever I visit, the predatory gangsters who lord over Gobabis' underbelly throng vulture-like round my truck and eyeball the cameras, camping equipment, GPS equipment, tools and other treasures packed into the back. Nor is it because perennial hunger and despair in Canaan find their expression in distended bellies, wounds that never seem to heal, or the deep wet tuberculotic coughs that seem to hang in the air long after the sound has passed—this happens in many other places too. Rather, it is because Canaan is so obviously the product of a series of technological, social, and economic forces that emanate from beyond Kalahari, forces that its Ju/'hoansi residents are powerless to affect even if, ironically, understanding how their parents and grandparents made a living as hunter-gatherers may well help us to manage those forces.

The "Primitive Affluence" of a Bygone Era

A CENTURY AGO THE JU/'HOANSI were undisputed masters of this desert land. But then white farmers and colonial police arrived with their horses, guns, water pumps, barbed wire and cattle. They soon crushed what little resistance the Ju/'hoansi offered and claimed this land for themselves. They also quickly learned that farming in the Kalahari Desert was labor-intensive. So they formed commandos to capture "wild Bushmen," held the Ju/'hoansi's children hostage to ensure their parents' obedience and meted out regular beatings to teach them the "virtues of hard work." Deprived of their traditional lands and regarded as "childlike creatures of the bush," Ju/'hoansi soon became dependent on the farmers for a place to stay and food to eat.

When Namibia gained its independence from South Africa in 1990, technological advances meant that the farms were more productive and less dependent on labor than they had ever been before. And with a new government demanding that farmers provide proper pay and housing for their workers, they reduced their workforces to the bare minimum, leaving many Ju/'hoansi and their dependents little option but to descend on squatter settlements like Canaan.

What happened on the Omaheke farms echoes broader trends transforming workplaces across the globe. Agriculture, manufacturing, and the services sector have been increasingly transformed by automation and, now, computerization. And as a slew of recent reports make clear, this trend is likely to accelerate.

For those not plagued by visions of a Terminator-style dystopia or in thrall to Jetson-like fantasies of hyper-modern convenience, the most pressing challenge raised by automation is the question of what people will do if there is not enough work to go around.

The same question also irked influential British economist John Maynard Keynes when in the winter of 1929 he was contemplating the ruins of his personal fortune. Global stock markets had imploded and the Great Depression was slowly throttling the life out of the transatlantic economy. To remind himself of the ephemeral nature of the crisis, he penned an optimistic essay entitled "The Economic

Possibilities for Our Grandchildren."[1] In it, he argued that within a century technical innovation and increases in productivity would usher in a golden era of leisure that would liberate us from the tyranny of the clock, and enable us to thrive on the basis of working no more than fifteen hours per week. Besides war, natural disasters, and acts of God, the only significant obstacle he saw to this Utopia being achieved was what he believed was our instinct to strive for more, to work and to create new wealth.

"We have been expressly evolved by nature—with all our impulses and deepest instincts—for the purpose of solving the economic problem," he lamented. "I think with dread of the readjustment of the habits and instincts of the ordinary man, bred into him for countless generations, which he may be asked to discard within a few decades." By "mankind's traditional purpose" Keynes was referring to our urge to work and produce; by the "economic problem" Keynes was referring to the "problem of scarcity" by which we work to bridge the gap between our infinite wants and limited means.

But Keynes believed economics to be a rational science and people, on the whole, to be capable of making rational choices when presented with them. So he took the view that,

---

1 John Maynard Keynes, "The Economic Possibilities for Our Grandchildren," in *Essays in Persuasion* (New York: W.W. Norton & Co., 1963), pp. 358-373. Essay first published in 1930.

save a few "purposeful money makers," we would recognize the economic Utopia for what it was, slow down and "be able to enjoy the abundance when it comes."

Keynes was right about improved productivity and technological innovation. They have been transformative, even more so than he imagined. According to his reasoning, on the basis of labor productivity improvements alone we should not be working more than eleven hours a week now. But he was wrong about the golden age of leisure. Despite having the means to work much less, many of us now work as long and hard as we did before. Keynes grossly underestimated just how hard it would be to readjust "the habits and instincts" of "ordinary" people.

Keynes was also wrong in imagining that a golden age of leisure could only come about through advances in productivity and technology. Convinced that mankind had been on a journey of unrelenting progress since the beginning of history, he saw the fifteen-hour week as the culmination of hundreds of generations' collective ingenuity and effort. What he failed to realize was that the fifteen-hour week was a reality for some of the handful of remaining tribes of autonomous hunter-gatherers, and that, in all probability, it was the norm for a significant proportion of the 200,000-year history of modern *Homo sapiens*.

But Keynes can be forgiven for this. During his lifetime there was no evidence to suggest that hunter-gatherer life was anything but "nasty, brutish, and short." The idea that hunter-gatherers led an easier life than he did would have seemed too absurd to take seriously.

In the 1960s, anthropologists considered the few Ju/'hoansi who still lived beyond the reach of the white ranchers to be the best living exemplars of how our hunting and gathering ancestors lived and so were chosen as the subjects of the first careful economic input/output studies of a hunting and gathering people—the results of which surprised everyone. Despite the harshness of their environment, the Ju/'hoansi made a good living on the basis of only between fifteen and seventeen hours' work per week. They spent the rest of their time on household chores, playing games, wooing lovers, crafting gifts, caring for children and telling stories.

Subsequent research showed how the Ju/'hoansi's relaxed approach to work stemmed from their faith in the providence of their environment and their confidence in their ability to exploit it—Ju/'hoansi made use of well over a hundred plant species and were adept at hunting pretty much anything that was edible. Consequently, the Ju/'hoansi had an "immediate return economy," which meant they never stored foods and only ever worked to procure enough to meet their short-term needs, certain that there was always more to be had with a few hours of effort. This research also demonstrated how the Ju/'hoansi's "fierce egalitarianism" underwrote their affluence by ensuring that resources flowed organically through communities, thus ensuring that even in the leanest times everyone got more or less enough.

Want Less, Work Less?

THE MOST COMPELLING ASPECT OF this research was that it suggested the "economic problem" was not, as Keynes believed, "the primary problem of the human race from the beginnings of time." For where the economic problem holds that we have unlimited wants and limited means, Ju/'hoansi hunter-gatherers had few wants that were easily satisfied. It was for this reason that Marshall Sahlins, arguably the most influential American social anthropologist of the twentieth century, redubbed hunter-gatherers "the original affluent society."[2]

Unsurprisingly, this simple idea briefly captured the popular imagination: "Imagine a society in which the work week seldom exceeds nineteen hours, material wealth is considered a burden, and no one is much richer than anyone else," gushed *Time* magazine in a November 1969 editorial about the Bushmen. "The people are comfortable, peaceable, happy, and secure ... This Elysian community actually exists."

---

2 Marshall Sahlins, "The Original Affluent Society," in *Stone Age Economics* (Chicago, Illinois: Aldine, Atherton, Inc., 1972), pp. 1–39.

But the idea of primitive affluence lost something of its broad appeal in the 1980s. The neoliberal economic revolution and the collapse of communism in Eastern Europe promised the world a new vision of capital-driven prosperity that left little room for apparently whimsical alternatives. Starved of mainstream attention, primitive affluence was left to be appropriated in a crude form by "new-age" movements seeking legitimacy for radical alternatives to mainstream culture.

Just as importantly, life for the Bushmen had also changed a great deal by the 1980s. Civil wars, forced relocations and the systematic colonization of large swathes of the Kalahari by white cattle ranchers and pastoralist tribes had transformed this "Elysian community" into an underclass. Anthropologists who ventured to the Kalahari encountered a people traumatized by changes that were beyond their control, often enslaved by their neighbors and alienated from the lands that had nurtured them for thousands of generations. Their plight was too dire and their lives too squalid and bereft of hope for anthropologists to wax lyrical about "primitive affluence." So they focused instead on the brutality of the Bushmen's encounter with others, the racism that justified their marginalization and the social and political structures that now looked set to pinion them into perpetual poverty.

And because anthropology tuned into these other aspects of their lives, the idea of "primitive affluence" fell out of favor. Some branded it a romantic myth. Others raised questions about the accuracy of some of the original data, pointing out that hunter-gatherers suffered from occasional hardships, that the fifteen-hour working week didn't apply equally to all hunter-gatherer groups, and that the data ignored time and effort spent on domestic tasks like preparing food and fires.

But in focusing their argument on these particular details, they conveniently ignored the central cultural pillar of the argument: that regardless of how many hours the Ju/'hoansi worked, they only worked to satisfy their immediate needs.

The early work on primitive affluence has recently been given new impetus by recent advances in genomics that have enabled us to map in increasingly greater detail the 200,000-year history of our species. These indicate that the northern Kalahari, rather than East Africa, may well have been the cradle of modern *Homo sapiens*. The data also suggests that this core group of *Homo sapiens* split into two around 150,000 years ago: while one branch gradually expanded northwards, colonizing the rest of the planet; the ancestors of the Bushmen remained where they were, so that by the time modern humans first set foot in South America 11,000 years ago the Bushmen had remained in the Kalahari for 140,000 years or more. Taken in tandem with a series of new archaeological finds, it also suggested that for at least 70,000 years—and possibly considerably more—the ancestors of modern Bushmen lived in the same places and in a very similar manner to those who were still hunting and gathering midway through the twentieth century. Perhaps most importantly, the data also reveals that if we measure the success of a civilization by its longevity, then the Bushmen were by far the most successful civilization in all of human history. Given that a society's ability to reproduce over time depends on its ability to feed itself, the key to the Bushmen's success lay in their economic approach.

When Keynes lamented the "habits and instincts bred into us over countless generations," he invoked a vision of human nature that almost certainly had its origins in the Agricultural Revolution — probably the most important turning point in the history our species. For while agriculture was far much more productive than hunting and gathering and enabled periods of rapid population growth, it also exposed these rapidly growing populations to a new range of catastrophic risk: from crop failure-induced famines to a series of new and terrifying diseases that migrated from their livestock. As a result, whereas hunter-gatherers like the Ju/'hoansi had an unyielding confidence in the providence of their environments, Neolithic farmers' lives were fraught with fear of droughts, blights, pests, diseases, famines, and later raids by equally stressed strangers.

The need to mitigate these risks inspired a range of wondrous social and technological innovations from food storage techniques to systems of trade and exchange. It also conveyed a distinct advantage to those that were able to control the production, storage and distribution of resources, thus giving rise to the problem of scarcity. At the same time, it placed an unprecedented premium on human labor. As any farmer will tell you, how much food you get out of your land depends on how much energy you put into it. The difference now, of course, is that most of this energy is automated.

With the Industrial Revolution now having merged into the Digital Revolution, there is a good case to be made that we have reached an inflexion point in the history of work as important as the Agricultural Revolution. Most of us in the world's richest countries enjoy lives of unparalleled material abundance. We are now so well-fed by the one percent of us who still work in agriculture that we throw roughly as much food into landfills every year as we consume. And with most of the rest of us working in the ever-more-amorphous services sector, much of the work we do is aimed at keeping wheels of commerce rolling rather than ensuring that our essential needs are met.

This would be fine if we had no reason to worry that our continued preoccupation with growth and keeping everybody endlessly productive risked cannibalizing our—and many other—species' future. It also would be fine if people like the Ju/'hoansi in Canaan had any realistic prospect of finding work. But with rural unemployment in Namibia sitting at 39.2 percent, this is unlikely in the foreseeable future not least because a byproduct of increasing productivity and automation is an economy in which capital drives growth more than does labor.

Yet most strategies proposed for dealing with problems like climate change and loss of biodiversity aim to find more sustainable ways for us to continue to produce, consume and work as much as we do. Likewise, most ideas proposed to manage automation's impact tend to focus mainly on the question of how to find replacement work for those nudged out by robots and artificial intelligence.

But if our working culture is an artifact of the Agricultural Revolution, and the economic problem has by and large been solved, then we should take comfort from several conclusions that we can draw from observing hunter-gatherers. Firstly, even if we are driven by purpose we are more than capable of leading contented lives that are not defined by our economic contributions. Secondly, automation provides exactly the opportunity we need to rethink our relationships with the workplace and in doing so wean ourselves off our dangerous obsession with growth.

This is of course easier said than done—as the Ju/'hoansi residents of Canaan know all too well. And if you were to ask those among them who still remember their lives as hunter-gatherers, they would remind you that their "primitive affluence" depended on far more than just a willingness to make do with having few needs easily met. It also demanded a society in which people cared little for accumulating wealth and in which everyone played an active role in jealously enforcing a fierce egalitarianism.

Ancient Forest
Scott T. Starbuck

People stare at iPhones
but what about listening

to voice of sea,
geese migrations,

salmon splashes,
cedar arms in wind,

like ages before
when men and women knew

quench soul hunger
first thing in morning

before saying anything
to anyone.

Letter to the Editor
Dr. Patrick L.

D ear Analog Sea Editors: I welcome your initiative. Poetry depends upon imagination and craft, and the digital world does little to enhance either. Inspiration is best savored; the process of quickening cannot be rushed. Larkin said you cannot will a poem into existence but I fear that digital processes encourage just that with inevitable consequences for quality of thought and execution.

Interview with Joseph-Antoine d'Ornano
Kyra Levine

T he beautifully evocative artworks that grace Analog Sea publications are the work of renowned Parisian painter and writer Joseph-Antoine d'Ornano, who has had a long collaboration with founder Jonathan Simons. Joseph has said that "the apparent simplicity of things often hides the unexpected." In experiencing his visual works, the observer is drawn to a seemingly simple landscape or scene, but on looking closer, one notices there is something else—something not pictured—a feeling, a sentiment, a connection. There is something that transcends the visual form and grabs the viewer's attention in the gentlest, yet most haunting way. I had the pleasure of sitting down for Sunday tea with Joseph in Paris to discuss the intention and process behind his works.

Joseph-Antoine d'Ornano strides with the familiarity of a regular over the threshold of a typically upscale Parisian hotel lobby in the 6th Arrondissement of Paris, in the Latin Quarter. It is a crisp, sunny spring afternoon, and when I met him fifteen minutes earlier in front of a nearby gallery where his paintings are on display, his first thought was not of showing me his works, but rather to ask if I were tired or needing sustenance after a long journey to reach him. "Are you hungry? It must have been a long trip, and such an early start this morning. Thank you for coming such a long way. I didn't know if you would like to have a late lunch, so I thought of a few options." I tell him that I'll be happy to just have a tea in a quiet place where we can talk freely, and with that, he was off, navigating the serpentine streets of Paris with ease, clearly knowing the neighborhood, "Like his pocket," as the French would say.

I lived in Paris for ten years, but never once found this gem just a few blocks south of the Seine. With a friendly "*bonjour*" and a knowing nod to the concierge, Joseph passes through the lobby and its classic, marble-topped bar, to the very back. As we enter I'm astonished to find myself in an exquisitely elegant, yet somehow surprisingly unpretentious tearoom, with seventeenth-century timber beams above our heads, a nod to the building's ancient footprint. Remarkably, we're alone. With all the teeming throngs of tourists just outside, I'm grateful we've managed to carve out a quiet, cozy spot where we can sit down and converse.

ANALOG SEA: We're here today because I wanted to meet you, to create this connection with you in person. Our little team at Analog Sea feels that in this changing world we need to create connection between human beings—on personal, artistic, and creative levels. So we'd like to explore your work and talk about what interests us, what attracts us. I'd firstly like to ask you about that statement that says so much: "The apparent simplicity of things often hides the unexpected." I find that very interesting.

JOSEPH-ANTOINE D'ORNANO: Well, in general I'm terrible at talking about painting! For me—and I've said this before—the criteria for a painting is: "Do I want this on my bedroom wall?" That's it. But then, in terms of whether there's a message, that's less interesting to me. What's essential is whether there's a closeness, a connection that one can have with a work.

AS: That's interesting, because just now on the train on the way here, I saw a quotation by the Indian writer and polymath Rabindranath Tagore: "Relationship is the fundamental truth of this world of appearance." What does that mean to you?

JO: You know, some people have a bit of a squint and I'm one of them. And someone who squints sees things a bit off from how others see them. What interests me is that I find life to be very rich. There are many things, and behind the appearances of, say, a courtyard or a house or a place like this, there is always some element of mystery for me. What I try to transpose into my writing or painting is something that arises from that reality. I'm not dealing with abstraction, but rather with a reality that is a little bit off; it's not a simply figurative reality. And it's that slightly off side that entails a mystery that I'm examining. Whether I express it or not, I don't know, but I'm looking into it. I feel that's enormously significant for me.

AS: That brings us to the question of inner and outer worlds, which is a topic that comes up for us so often.

JO: Absolutely, yes. It's not about simply transposing something. It's about really entering into that which is mysterious … life is mysterious, people are mysterious! [laughs]

AS: That's for sure!

JO: And I think that's what it comes down to. When Rainer Maria Rilke saw the first abstract paintings, he said something like "I won't say anything, but I'm not too optimistic." He said that! He must have suspected that it could really drift off into something that wasn't particularly interesting, precisely because that's what happens when one moves away from all sense of reality and mystery.

AS: I also notice a strong sense of spirituality in your œuvre. That's perhaps something very personal for each individual, but it's something that jumps out at me from your visual works—a spirit, a creation, a relation that one can observe with something that isn't actually there.

JO: What I really like to see in a sketch is a sense of grace—that is, the realization that it doesn't all depend on us. There's an element of the unexpected, an element that goes beyond us. And once one goes beyond the sketch and attempts to achieve a [complete] painting, our will, our work becomes involved—everything depends on us, and it's less interesting for me. I'm more about the strokes, the sketches. Because I think in that, there is a relation with the transcendent, and that's the unexpected.

AS: In an interview some years ago you mentioned that you had recently revisited "Bartleby the Scrivener"[1] and the works of Camus. You said that Bartleby made you want to write, and that while *The Stranger* didn't touch you the first time, on that later read you saw a connection between all beings and everything that happens. Both of those statements really interested me because they aren't, well ... they're not quite the concepts being put forth in the text.

JO: Well, this "I would prefer not" is a very strong statement. But I coined this word, *irreference*: that is, that which has no reference. Because there's a link between a character like Bartleby, like *The Stranger*, like the fact of uncertainty ... all that for me, is a connection with truth. I go around and around it, and I haven't arrived, of course, but I think that it's a path not to be avoided. One must work toward it. And the

---

1 Herman Melville, "Bartleby," in *The Piazza Tales* (New York: Dix & Edwards, 1866). First published anonymosly as "Bartleby, the Scrivener: A Story of Wall Street" in *Putnam's Magazine* in 1853.

major problem we're facing today, and it's related to Aristotle, is that people think that opinion is fact …

AS: … fake news! It's everywhere!

JO: Yes, and that's the problem! I have an opinion, you have an opinion, I believe this, you believe that and that must mean there are two truths. No! There can only be one truth. What it is, I don't know, but let's at least agree that there's only one. But we can't even manage that, because often people say, "my truth is the truth." Even if I just think it is. You can say to someone, "Do people live on Mars?" and they'll answer, "Well I think people live on Mars"; another will say, "I don't think people live on Mars," so there are two truths. That's not possible! It's one or the other. And that's what Aristotle did with the Sophists.

AS: It makes me think of the second chapter of your book *On the Origins of Contemporary Violence* in which you talk about quantum mechanics …

JO: Well, I wrote that a long time ago …

AS: … and the principle of uncertainty, as well as the actual observation of uncertainty. To establish certainty, the external observer must precisely determine both the position and the speed of a particle at the exact same time. It's impossible! And that comes down to the instrument of observation for this type of a posteriori experience—and that's the same thing for human beings, because the very instrument of observation is the human being, it's the mind.

JO: Of course! And for example I feel that with all these machines, the computer and all this stuff—the body is absent. The body is no longer there, so when you talk to someone it's like … you're talking to …

AS: It's a decapitated relationship.

JO: Yes. It's a relationship in which the body no longer exists. We're more and more in a place where there's content all over, but it contains nothing. It's going to lead us into more stuff, and make things worse long-term. What's the solution? I don't know, but there's some relationship with spirituality there, I'm sure. We're going through a crisis of aesthetics nowadays. There's progress in the field of medicine, there's progress here, there, you name it. But when it comes to beauty, we're in total crisis. It's as if everything is inverted; it's an apologia for ugliness. The bad—in taste, not in moral connotation—the bad, the false, becomes the reference. It is clear that certain trends of evolution today are moving toward a civilization connected to killing things, negating life. I'm struck by artworks in which, for example, faces are absent, bodies are absent, landscapes are gone: everything in nature is absent, and there's this vindication of the quotidian [absence]. Maybe I'm a bit reactionary. But people don't realize that the true subversion is classicism.

That doesn't mean we have to go back to the past, but to what's serious. For example, I take poetry seriously. Poetry is not anodyne. Poetry, music, art—these are very serious things, but today there is some sense of them being a game. We are still living in a civilization of derision. There's derision everywhere. It never stops. And that's not good. We need to come back to a certain gravity. Yet some people just want to be shocked. There's a major art collector I know of who says, "Artwork has to shock me as soon as I see it and it has to be ugly to shock me." If you say, "I'd like to see something harmonious," people say, "What's wrong with this old geezer?" It's this sort of inversion that characterizes our society, our civilization.

AS: That brings me back to the main argument in your book about violence. I'm reminded of Mark Kurlansky's book *Nonviolence: The History of a Dangerous Idea*, in which he writes: "The first clue, lesson number one from human history on the subject of nonviolence is that there is no word for it. Throughout history there have been practitioners of nonviolence. Yet, while every major language has a word for violence, there is no word to express the idea of nonviolence except that it is not another idea, it is not violence." How does that strike you?

JO: In my book I tried to find a common denominator, and it's the rupture of connection at every level. It's on the personal level, but also in places that no longer necessarily have any connection between them. It's trite to speak of urban and suburban issues, but this is a discontinuity that exists in actual places, and in everything that happens to us, especially in the nature of violence. That's the crux of the book: today, violence is not connected to a particular thing. It's violence that is gratuitous. There are classic examples of violence that can be traced to a cause, but I think what's new today is the appearance of forms of violence that are not at all connected to one specific object. This lack of connection is present everywhere: among people, in art, in everything that happens in society today, either because things are separated or because they are fused. One example is the virtual and the real: they have become one thing, so there's no more establishing what's outer and what's inner, they're coexisting simultaneously.

AS: It seems like everything is inverted. The banal is the miraculous, the miraculous is the banal. I especially have that impression in the United States, being from there originally.

JO: Precisely! But everything that was happening in the U.S. fifteen, twenty years ago is happening in France today.

AS: It seems to be a mirror showing us the direction things are going but I don't know what's the chicken or what's the egg in this scenario.

JO: Absolutely. It's the chicken and the egg. But I think if you feel that inversion, if you turn that around, then it must mean that something true exists. You see? Because if you invert the inversion, you can re-establish the equilibrium. And that's why I think truth exists.

AS: So maybe there is some silver lining in all these clouds, as we'd say in English.

JO: Yes, and that's where transcendence comes in. Art needs to raise us up.

AS: It brings us back to how we don't want to see where we are and see the speed at which we're going at the same time; we're looking backwards and forwards yet we don't know where we are.

JO: Precisely.

AS: It's really a challenge particular to humans. I remember when I did a Vipassana meditation retreat a few years ago, it was ten or twelve hours of meditation per day, for ten days, in silence. There were no distractions, no books, no pens, no paper, no phone, no anything. I remember hearing the teacher, S.N. Goenka, say that ninety-five percent of our thoughts are on the past or the future, and only about five percent on what is really happening …

JO: … in the present.

AS: Exactly.

JO: You know, it is said that birds never worry about what they'll eat tomorrow. They know that there will always be something; they're in the present. And if we had that total trust, imagine what great things we'd create! We'd live in the present, without worry.

JOSEPH AND I KEEP CONVERSING, and I have the feeling we could talk all day over several more pots of tea, with the Sunday afternoon sun gently streaming through the windows until Joseph suddenly looks at his watch and says with genuine concern, "Oh my, your train! I don't want you to leave, but you mustn't miss your train!"

We say our warm goodbyes, and I feel I've truly connected with a new friend. Before heading toward the Gare du Nord to catch my train, I discover that Joseph has added one final touch of class to this lovely afternoon—he picked up the check without my even noticing.

A number of Joseph-Antoine d'Ornano's works feature in the permanent collection of the Galerie Grillon in Paris, which has organized temporary exhibitions of his works at art fairs in the Grand Palais, Paris and in New York. Selected items are also currently exhibited at the Peinture Fraîche Gallery in Paris and the Olivier Rousseau Gallery of Tours, Loire Valley. Among his works of fiction are *Côté chambre coté jardin*, *La résidence*, and *Le visage flou de Steiner*; his nonfiction works include *Essai sur l'origine de la violence contemporaine* (*On the Origins of Contemporary Violence*) and *Essai sur le principe d'irreference: L'homme a la recherche du sens* (*On the Principle of Irreference: Man and the Search for Meaning*).

There Is a Vitality
Martha Graham

There is a vitality, a life force, an energy, a quickening that is translated through you into action, and because there is only one of you in all time, this expression is unique. And if you block it, it will never exist through any other medium and will be lost. The world will not have it. It is not your business to determine how good it is, nor valuable, nor how it compares with other expression. It is your business to keep it yours clearly and directly, to keep the channel open. You do not even have to believe in yourself or your work. You have to keep yourself open and aware to the urges that motivate you. *Keep the channel open.*

Quoted in Agnes de Mille, *Martha: The Life and Work of Martha Graham* (New York: Random House, 1991), p. 264.

The London Library
E.M. Forster

I n May 1841 the London Library was launched on the
swelling tides of Victorian prosperity. It celebrates its
centenary among the rocks. It is unharmed at the moment of
writing—not a volume out of action—but the area in which
it stands is cloven by the impacts of the imbecile storm. All
around it are the signs of the progress of science and the ret-
rogression of man. Building are in heaps, the earth is in holes.
Safe still among the reefs of rubbish, it seems to be something
more than a collection of books. It is a symbol of civilization.
It is a reminder of sanity and a promise of sanity to come.
Perhaps the Nazis will hit it, and it is an obvious target, for it
represents the tolerance and the disinterested erudition which
they so detest. But they have missed it so far.[1]

Why should a private subscription library, which appeals
to only a small section of the community, arouse exalted
thoughts? The answer to this question is to be found in the
Library's history, and in its present policy. Speakers at its
annual meetings are fond of saying that it is unique, which is
more or less true, and that it is typically English, which greatly
understates its claims. It is not typically English. It is typically
civilized. It pays a homage to seriousness and to good sense
which is rare in these islands and anywhere. It has cherished

---

1 They hit it in 1944.

the things of the mind, it has insisted on including all points of view, and yet it has been selective. Ephemeral books, popular successes, most novels, many travelogues, and biographies have been excluded from its shelves. And technical treatises, such as have helped to make the mess outside, have not been encouraged either. Of course it has had its lapses; one can find trash in it, and specialization—lumber also. But its policy has always been to send those who want trash to the chain-libraries, and those who want lumber to their appropriate lumber-room. It caters neither for the goose nor for the rat, but for creatures who are trying to be human. The desire to know more, the desire to feel more, and, accompanying these but not strangling them, the desire to help others: here, briefly, is the human aim, and the Library exists to further it.

So much for its seriousness. Its good sense is equally remarkable. For it would be possible to have these admirable ideals, but to render them unacceptable through red tape. That is the great snag in institutionalism. There may be fine intention and noble provision, but they often get spoiled by the belief that the public cannot be trusted, that it is careless, dishonest, grubby, clumsy, that it must on no account be "allowed access" to the shelves, and its best serves from behind a wire netting. The London Library, though an institution, will have nothing to do with this fallacy. It takes the risks. Its members can go all over its bookstores. There is a price to be paid; books do get stolen, or taken out without being entered, or taken out in unauthorized quantities, or kept out too long, or dogs-eared, or annotated in the margin by cultivated scribes who should know better; but it is worth it, it is worth treating the creatures as if they were grown up, the gain to the humanities outweighs the financial loss. Moreover, it is the tradition of the library to help the student rather than to snub, and this promotes a decent reaction at once. And "help" is indeed too feeble a word; the officials there possess not only good-will, but wide and accurate knowledge, which is instantly placed at the enquirer's disposal.

The library owes its origin to the spleen and the nobility of Thomas Carlyle. The spleen came first; Carlyle needed books of reference while he was writing his *Cromwell*, he could not afford to buy them all, and the journey from Chelsea to the British Museum Library was a vexatious one. Besides, when he got to the British Museum he found other people reading there too, which gave him the feeling of a crowd, and it is impossible to work in a crowd: "add discomfort, perturbation, headache, waste of health." Grumbling and growling at his miserable fate, he betook himself to the drawing-room of Lady Stanley of Alderley in Dover Street, and burst forth there; even in Iceland, he said, the peasants could borrow books, and take them away to read in their huts during the Arctic night; only in London was there this "shameful anomaly." The company tried to soothe him or to change the subject, but his growls continued; books, books, one ought to be able to borrow books. And before long, he effected of his junctions between private peevishness and public welfare, and persuaded other men of distinction to combine with him in launching a library. Gladstone, Hallam, Grote, Monckton Milnes joined him. A meeting was held at the Freeman's Tavern to promote a scheme for "a supply of good books in all departments of knowledge." Lord Eliot was in the chair, and Carlyle made a fine speech. It is said to be his only speech. Here are some sentences from it:

> A book is a kind of thing which requires a man to be self-collected. He must be alone with it. A good book is the purest essence of the human soul… The good of a book is not the facts that can be got out of it, but the kind of resonance that it awakes in our own minds. A book may strike out a thousand things which it does not know itself… The founding of a Library is one of the greatest things we can do with regard to results. It is one of the quietest of things; but there is nothing that I know of at bottom more important. Everyone able to read a good book becomes a wiser man. He becomes a similar centre of light and order, and just insight into the things around him. A collection of good books contains all the nobleness and wisdom of the world before us. Every heroic and victorious soul has left this stamp upon it. A collection of books is the best of all Universities; for the University only teaches us to read the book: you must go to the book

itself for what it is. I call it a Church also—which every
devout soul may enter—a Church but with no quarreling,
no Church-rates…

At this point, Carlyle was interrupted by laughter and cheers,
and sat down good-temperedly. His speech is too optimistic,
in view of our present information; also too subjective in its
emphasis on the "resonance" from books; also too little aware
of the power of concentration possessed by many readers,
which enables them today to continue through an air-raid.
But it is a noble utterance. It recalls us to the importance of
seriousness, and to the preciousness and the destructibility
of knowledge. Knowledge will perish if we do not stand up
for it and testify. It is never safe, never harvested. It has to
be protected not only against the gangster but against a much
more charming and seductive foe: the crowd. "I know what
I like and I know what I want," says the crowd, "and I don't
want all these shelves and shelves of books. Scrap them."

The Library started in two rooms at 49 Pall Mall, with
five hundred members, and three thousand books. Conditions
were Spartan; no ink or paper was provided, and for a time
there was no clock. In 1845 it moved into St. James's Square,
and now it has a membership of four thousand and about
four hundred and seventy thousand books, together with
various luxuries, including a comfortable reading-room. Its
rise is largely due to a great librarian, Sir Charles Hagberg

Wright, who died last year. Hagberg Wright had a European connection, and a European outlook. He was free from the insularity which has such a numbing effect on the collecting of books, and it is largely thanks to him that one feels the library to be not English but civilized. For the moment it has one overwhelming problem before it: that of not getting smashed and not getting burnt. But if normality returns it will have the task of getting into touch with the thought and literature of the Continent, however repellent the mental state of the Continent may be. And—a more congenial task—it will have to get up to date on America. It has never admitted, and it must never admit, the idea of exclusion; in Hagberg Wright's wise little pamphlet, *The Soul's Dispensary*, there are some pertinent remarks on this, and a curious account of the war which he had to wage after the last war with various government departments before he could regain liberty for the reimportation of foreign literature.

E.M. Forster, "The London Library," from *Two Cheers for Democracy* (London: Edward Arnold, 1972), pp. 299–302. Essay first published in *The New Statesman and Nation* in 1941.

Lunch
Steven Doloff

A flock of pigeons circles and flutters to the ground in the smallest park in the largest city in the world. As they pass along the pavement into the shade of the trees, I sense the whole human business come to an end, and the soft noise of feathers takes dominion. The breath and fret of multitudes melt upon the wind. The concrete bones rest in the air. The iron blood is quiet in its cavernous veins. In the stillness and the light, I am anointed by the murmur of birds. I chew my sandwich. I sip my coffee. A breeze rises from the ground and brushes the leaves. I look, and the pigeons clap into the air. Like gems upon a vanishing wizard's sleeve, they sweep round and over the trees and are gone. I turn, and it rains again the honk and bustle of things.

Vita Contemplativa
Byung-Chul Han

A Brief History of Leisure

Heidegger is said to have opened one of his lectures on Aristotle by saying: "Aristotle was born, worked, and died."[1] It is surprising that Heidegger would characterize Aristotle's life as work. He must have known that the life of a philosopher—as a *bios theoretikos*—was anything but work. According to Aristotle, philosophizing—as *theorein*—owes its existence to leisure (*schole*). The meaning of the Greek *schole* has little to do with today's "idleness" or "leisure time." It is a state of freedom, without coercion or necessitation, without toil or care. Work, by contrast, takes away freedom, because it is subject to the coercive force exerted by the necessities of life. As opposed to leisure, it does not rest in itself, because it must produce what is useful and necessary.

Aristotle divided life into two areas, into time employed for non-leisure (*a-scholia*) and time of leisure (*schole*), that is, into non-rest and rest. Work as non-rest, as un-freedom, must be subordinated to leisure. With regard to activities (*prakta*), Aristotle also situated the beautiful and noble outside of what

---

1 Hannah Arendt and Martin Heidegger, *Letters 1925–1975*, trans. Andrew Shields (Orlando, Florida: Harcourt, 2004), p. 154.

is useful and necessary, that is, outside of work.[2] Only need forces work upon us; work is therefore *need*-ful. Leisure, by contrast, opens up a space beyond the necessities of life that is free of compulsion and care. According to Aristotle, the nature of human existence is not care, but leisure. Contemplative rest enjoys absolute priority. All activities have to be carried out with the aim of this rest in mind and have to return to it.

Aristotle distinguishes three forms of life (*bioi*) of the *free* man: the life of striving for pleasure (*hedone*), that of producing beautiful and noble deeds in the polis (*bios politikos*), and that which is dedicated to the contemplation of truth (*bios theoretikos*).[3] All three of them are free from the needs and compulsions of life. The life dedicated to making money is set aside on account of its compulsive character. The *bios politikos* is not dedicated to the organization of communal life, because this would involve man in necessary and useful things. Rather, it strives for honor and virtue. Skills such as drawing and painting are to be acquired because they promote the ability to contemplate physical beauty.[4] The highest form of happiness has its source in the contemplative lingering on beauty, the activity that used to be called *theoria*. Its temporal dimension

2 Aristotle, *Politics*, trans. Sir Ernest Barker (Oxford: Oxford University Press, 1995), p. 1333a.

3 Aristotle, *Nicomachean Ethics,* trans. Roger Crisp (Cambridge: Cambridge University Press, 2000), p. 6f.

4 Aristotle, *Politics*, p. 300f.

is duration. It turns towards those things that are imperishable and unchanging, the things that rest entirely in themselves. Only the contemplative devotion to truth, not virtue and not prudence, brings man close to the gods.

Leisure, being *schola*, is outside of work and outside of inactivity. It is a special ability and requires a specific education. It is not a practice of "relaxation" or of "switching off." Thinking, as *theorein*, as the contemplative consideration of truth, is based on leisure. Thus, St Augustine distinguishes leisure (*otium*) from passive inertia: "The attraction of a life of leisure ought not to be the prospect of a lazy inactivity, but the chance for the investigation and discovery of truth." The "praiseworthy kind of leisure" entails "the pursuit of truth."[5] The incapacity for leisure is precisely a sign of inertia. Leisure is not the neighbor of lazy inactivity; it is its opposite. It does not serve the purpose of distraction, but of collecting oneself. Lingering presupposes a gathering of the senses.

In the Middle Ages, *vita contemplativa* still maintained priority over *vita activa*. Thus, Aquinas wrote: "*Vita contemplativa simpliciter melior est quam activa*" [the contemplative life is simply more excellent than the active].[6] The well-known dictum *ora et labora* does not express an appreciation of work

---

5 Saint Augustine, *City of God,* trans. Henry Bettenson (London: Penguin, 1984), p. 880.

6 Thomas Aquinas, *Summa Theologica II*, trans. Fathers of the English Dominican Province (Novantiqua, 2014), p. 427.

over contemplation. In the Middle Ages, the *vita activa* was still altogether imbued with the *vita contemplativa*. Work was given its meaning by contemplation. The day began with prayers. And prayers ended it. They provided a temporal rhythm. An altogether different significance attached to the festive days. They were not days off work. As times of prayer and of leisure they had their own significance. The medieval calendar did not just serve the purpose of *counting* days. Rather, it was based on a *story* in which the festive days represent narrative resting points. They are fixed points within the flow of time, providing narrative bonds so that the time does not simply elapse. The festive days form temporal sections which structure time and give it a rhythm. They function like the sections of a story, and let time and its passing appear meaningful. Each section of a story completes a narrative section, and this provisional completion prepares the next stage of the narrative. The temporal sections are meaningful transitions within an overall narrative frame. The time of hope, the time of joy, and the time of farewell merge into each other.

The attitude towards work begins to change in the late Middle Ages. Thomas More's *Utopia*, for instance, paints a picture of a world in which everyone works. His revolutionary project for a new society is aimed against class distinctions and suggests a just distribution of work. Everyone needs to work for only six hours every day. In their time away from work, the "utopians" dedicate themselves to leisure and contemplation. But the value of work as such is not actually increased by this design. Only in the context of the Reformation does work acquire an importance which far exceeds that of fulfilling the necessities of life. It is now put in the context of a theological meaning that serves to legitimate it and raise its value. In Luther, work as a vocation is associated with God's calling upon men. In Calvinism, work is given meaning in the context of the economy of salvation. A Calvinist is uncertain whether or not he or she is chosen or condemned. Thus, anxiety and permanent care [*Sorge*] dominate the acting of the individual, who is left entirely to his own devices. Only success in work is interpreted as a sign of having been chosen. The care for salvation turns the individual into a worker. Although this restless labor cannot achieve salvation, it is the only means of assuring oneself of having been chosen, and thus of reducing anxiety.

Calvinism develops an emphasis on acting and on determined activity: "The religious believer can make himself sure of his state of grace *either* in that he feels himself to be the vessel of the Holy Spirit or the tool of the divine will. In the former case his religious life tends to mysticism and emotionalism, in the latter to ascetic action."[7] A Calvinist attains the certainty of his salvation by acting with resolve. The seeker of

---

7 Max Weber, *The Protestant Ethic and the Spirit of Capitalism*, trans. R.H. Tawney (Kettering, Ohio: Angelicopress, 2014), p. 68.

salvation is brought closer to his goal not by a *vita contemplativa*, but by a *vita activa*. With the raising of the determination to act to the level of an absolute value, the *vita contemplativa* appears reprehensible.

The inner-worldly asceticism of Protestantism connects work with salvation. Work increases the glory of God. It becomes the purpose of life. Max Weber quotes the Pietist Zinzendorf: "One does not only work in order to live, but one lives for the sake of one's work, and if there is no more work to do one suffers or goes to sleep."[8] Wasting time is the worst of all sins. Extending the hours of sleep unnecessarily is also condemned. The economy of time and that of salvation become intermingled.

THE WORD "INDUSTRY" DERIVES FROM the Latin term *industria*, which means "diligence." The English word "industry" retains the meaning of "diligence" and "busy activity" to the present day. "Industrial School," for instance, meant "reformatory." Industrialization not only meant the mechanization of the world, but also the disciplining of human beings. It installed not only machines, but also dispositifs that optimized human behavior, even optimized the physical body itself, in the interest of temporal and labor efficiency. Typically enough, a treatise of 1768 by Philipp Peter Guden

---

8 Ibid., n. 24, p. 166.

is called "Polizey der Industrie, oder Abhandlung von den Mitteln, den Fleiß der Einwohner zu ermuntern" [The policing of industry, or: treatise on the means for encouraging the diligence of inhabitants].

With the process of industrialization as mechanization, human temporality approaches the temporality of machines. The industrial dispositif is an imperative of temporal efficiency that has the task of forming the human being according to the timing of the machine. It aligns human life to the mechanical working process—to functioning. Life dominated by work is a *vita activa*, which is entirely cut off from the *vita contemplativa*. If the human being loses all capacity for contemplation, it degenerates into an *animal laborans*. The life which adjusts itself to the mechanical work process knows only breaks, work-free interim periods in which the regeneration from work takes place in order to be fully available again for the process of work. Thus, "relaxation" and "switching off" do not constitute a counterbalance to work. They are integrated into the work process, in the sense that they primarily serve the purpose of re-establishing the ability to work.

The so-called society of leisure and consumption does not bring about an essential change in work. It is not free from the imperative to work. The source of the compulsion is, in this case, no longer the necessities of life but work itself. Hannah Arendt erroneously assumes that the telos of the society of laborers is the freedom of the human being from the "fetters" of labor.[9] In reality, this society is one in which labor, independent of the necessities of life, becomes an end in itself and posits itself as absolute. Work is totalized to such a degree that outside of working hours the only time that remains is that which is to be "killed." The totalization of labor pushes out all other forms of life and life projects. It forces the mind itself to work. "Intellectual labor" is a formula of compulsion. The *mind* that works would be a contradiction.

The society of consumption and leisure is characterized by a particular temporality. Surplus time, which is the result of a massive increase in productivity, is filled with events and experiences that are fleeting and short-lived. As nothing binds time in a lasting fashion, the impression is created that time is passing very quickly, or that everything is accelerating. Consumption and duration contradict each other. Consumer goods do not last. They are marked by decay as their constitutive element, and the cycles of appearance and decay become ever shorter. The capitalist imperative of growth means that things are produced and consumed with increasing speed. The compulsion to consume is immanent to the system of production. Economic growth depends on the quick uptake and consumption of things. As the economy is organized with growth in mind, it would completely grind to a halt if people

9 Hannah Arendt, *The Human Condition* (Chicago and London: University of Chicago Press, 1958), p. 5.

suddenly began to take care of things, to protect them against decay and to make sure that they endure.

In the consumer society, one forgets how to linger. Consumer goods do not permit a contemplative lingering. They are used up as quickly as possible in order to create space for new products and needs. Contemplative lingering presupposes things which endure. But the compulsion to consume does away with duration. Neither, however, does so-called deceleration found duration. As far as the attitude to consumption is concerned, "slow food" does not essentially differ from "fast food." Things are consumed—no more, no less. A reduction in speed does not by itself transform the *being* of things. The real problem is that all that endures, all that lasts and is slow, threatens to disappear altogether, or to be absent from life. Forms of the *vita contemplativa* are also modes of being, such as "hesitancy," "releasement," "shyness," "waiting," or "restraint," which the later Heidegger juxtaposed to the "stupidity of simply working."[10] These modes all rest on an experience of duration. But the time of work, even time as work, is without duration. It *consumes* time for production. What lasts and is slow, however, evades being used up and consumed. It founds a duration. The *vita contemplativa*

---

10 Martin Heidegger, "The Pathway," trans. Thomas F. O'Meara, *Listening* 8 (1973), pp. 37.

is a practice of duration. It founds an *other time* by interrupting the *time of work*.

Vita Contemplativa, or of Reflective Life

All of you, to whom unrestrained labor, and the swift, the new, the strange, are dear, you endure yourselves ill, your industry is flight and will to forget yourselves. — *Friedrich Nietzsche*[11]

THINKING, ARENDT REMARKS IN *The Human Condition*, has always been the privilege of the few. But just for that very reason, they have not become even fewer today.[12] However, this assumption is not entirely correct. It may be a particular characteristic of the present that thinkers, anyhow a small number at any time, have become even fewer. Thinking might have suffered from the fact that the *vita contemplativa* has been pushed aside in favor of the *vita activa*; it is possible that the hyperactive restlessness, the franticness and unrest of today, does not do any good to thinking, and that thinking just reproduces always the same because of increasing time pressures.

---

11 Friedrich Nietzsche, *Thus Spoke Zarathustra*. trans. Reg Hollingdale (London: Penguin, 1969), p. 73.

12 Translators note: The passage runs: "As a living experience, thought has always been assumed, perhaps wrongly, to be known only to the few. It may not be presumptuous to believe that these few have not become fewer in our time."

Nietzsche already lamented the poverty of his times regarding great thinkers, and he explained this poverty with the "decline and occasional underestimation of the *vita contemplativa*," with the fact "that work and industry (formerly attending the great goddess of Health) sometimes seem to rage like a disease." Because there is "no time for thinking, and no rest in thinking,"[13] divergent views are avoided. They are just hated. The general restlessness does not allow thinking to go deep, to venture far, really to reach for something genuinely different. It is not thinking that dictates to time, but time that dictates to thinking, making it temporary and ephemeral. Thinking no longer communicates with that which lasts. However, Nietzsche believed that "when the genius of meditation makes a powerful return," this will let his lament fall silent.[14]

Thinking, in the emphatic sense, cannot be accelerated at will. That is where it differs from calculating or from the pure use of the understanding. It often moves in roundabout ways. This is why Kant called wit and acumen "a kind of intellectual luxury." The understanding is only concerned with needs and necessity, but not with luxury, which represents a deviation from necessity, even from all things *straight and direct*. A special temporality and spatiality is intrinsic to thinking

---

13 Friedrich Nietzsche, *Human, All Too Human*, trans. Marion Faber (London: Faber, 1994), p. 170.

14 Ibid., p. 171.

that rises above calculating. It does not progress in linear fashion. Thinking is free because its place and time cannot be calculated. It often progresses discontinuously, while calculating follows a linear path. Thus, calculating can be precisely located and, in principle, accelerated at will. Calculating does not look around either. For it, a detour or a step back do not make sense. They only delay the step in the calculation, which is purely a step of the work process. Today, thinking assimilates itself to labor. However, the *animal laborans* is incapable of thinking. For thinking in the emphatic sense, pensive thinking [*sinnendes Denken*], something is required that is not work. Originally, *Sinnen* [Old High German *sinnan*] meant "journeying" [*Reisen*]. Its *itinerary* is incalculable or discontinuous. Calculating thought is not on the way.

Without rest human beings are incapable of seeing what is at rest. Making the *vita activa* an absolute value drives everything out of life that is not an act or activity. The general time pressures destroy all that has the character of a detour, all that is indirect, and thus makes the world poor in forms. Every form, every figure, is a *detour*. Only naked formlessness is direct. If language is deprived of what is indirect in it, its nature approaches that of a scream or an order. Friendliness and politeness are also based on the circuitous and indirect. The orientation of violence, by contrast, is towards directness. If walking lacks all hesitation, all pausing, then it freezes into a march. Time pressures also make what is ambivalent and undecidable, what hovers—the complex or aporetic—give way to a crude distinctness. Nietzsche remarks that the haste of work also makes "the ear and eye for the melody of movements" disappear.[15] A melody is a detour. Only what is monotonous is direct. Thinking is also marked by a melody. Thinking that entirely lacks any circuitous character degenerates into calculating.

The *vita activa*, which, since the beginning of modern times, has become more and more intense at the expense of the *vita contemplativa*, contributes substantially to the modern compulsion to accelerate. The degradation of the human being to an *animal laborans* can also be interpreted as an effect of this modern development. The emphasis on labor and on acting are *both* based on the primacy of the *vita activa* in modern times and modernity. But Arendt's sharp separation of labor from acting, by interpreting labor as a passive participation in the life of the species, is unjustified. Her concept of acting lacks the evocative power that would have the capacity to break the spell of labor, which degrades the human being to an *animal laborans*, because her emphatic concept of labor is derived from the same primacy of the *vita activa* from which the absolute value of labour is *also* derived. As has repeatedly been stressed, the determination to act and the determination to work share

---

15 Friedrich Nietzsche, *The Gay Science*, trans. Josefine Nauckhoff (Cambridge: Cambridge University Press, 2001), p. 184.

the same genealogical root. Only a revitalization of the *vita contemplativa* would be capable of liberating human beings from the compulsion to labor. In addition, the *animal laborans* is related to the *animal rationale* because the pure exercise of the faculty of understanding is labor. The human being, however, is more than an animal because it possesses the capacity for contemplation, which enables it to communicate with that which lasts, and which, however, does not constitute a class [*Gattung*].

ACCORDING TO THOMAS AQUINAS, THE *vita contemplativa* represents a form of life which makes the human being more perfect: "*In vita contemplativa quaeritur contemplatio veritatis inquantum est perfectio hominis*" [in the contemplative life the contemplation of truth is sought as being the perfection of man].[16] The *vita contemplativa* elevates time itself. As opposed to Arendt's claim, there is no one-sided appreciation of the *vita contemplativa* in the Christian tradition.

A *vita contemplativa* without acting is blind, a *vita activa* without contemplation is empty.

If all contemplative elements are driven out of life, it ends in a deadly hyper-activity. The human being suffocates among its *own* doings. What is necessary is a revitalization of the *vita contemplativa*, because it opens up spaces for breathing. Perhaps

---

16 Thomas Aquinas, *Summa Theologica II*, q. 180, a. 4, p. 400.

the mind itself owes its emergence to an excess of time, an *otium*, even to a slowness of breath. A reinterpretation of *pneuma*, which means breath as well as spirit, is conceivable. Whoever runs out of breath is without spirit. The democratization of work must be followed by a democratization of *otium*, lest the former turn into the bondage of everyone. Thus, Nietzsche writes:

> From lack of rest, our civilization is ending in a new barbarism. Never have the active, which is to say the restless, people been prized more. Therefore, one of the necessary correctives that must be applied to the character of humanity is a massive strengthening of the contemplative element.[17]

---

17 Friedrich Nietzsche, *Human, All Too Human*, p. 172.

Adapted from Byung-Chul Han, "Vita Contemplativa" in *The Scent of Time: A Philosophical Essay on the Art of Lingering,* trans. Daniel Steuer (Cambridge: Polity Press, 2017), pp. 85–114.

The Light Is Different There
Lesley Saunders

1.
We think we know them, the ancient Greeks,
their luminous roofless temples and conversational
market-places under the unblinking southern light;

we imagine we owe it all to them, our love lyrics
and war music, our tragedies and democracies
(even the tragedy of our democracy); the children

we name Helen, Alexander; or the come-uppance
for hubris, the nemesis we swerve to escape,
and the inevitable displacement of water

by the brute matter-of-fact of our mortal bodies.
That day I arrived by coach in central Athens
with a rucksack and sleeping-bag I'd used as pillow

down the three-day length of the Yugoslav *autoput*,
I bedded down with a dozen others on a hotel roof
under the stars, whose white heat in the stove of the city

seared through my eyelids, burning out sleep.
The hostel I'd fled from was flea-ridden, filthy,
and by the Parthenon a man tried to grab my breast:

but Sappho had surely taught us all we need to know
about sleepless nights, the absent lover's touch, the sweet
ache of solitude—she wrote in fragments, did she not,

so we could fill the spaces with our own disconsolations?
When I came to Delphi, the air was thick with scents
and cicadas, a sharpish fragrance I couldn't place,

a sound that seemed to hold inside it an ageless kind
of menace, mocking even when it briefly stopped:
Theokritos it wasn't, the idyll-days of wine and roses

were always in another poem I hadn't written,
a goat sang outside the stable-door of the shack
I slept in, and the cockerel was relentless with his hens.

What I hadn't realised in those homesick days
was the truthfulness of my anxiety, the utter lack
of fit between ideal and real, and how pity and terror

make sense not as abstractions but only as openings into
the dark ground where the matted creature crouches
and hisses out the stinking blasphemous words of god.

II.

No-one else was on the platform at Larisa railway station
when I arrived with hours to kill. The waiting-room, stilled
to an echoless chamber, became a this-and-only-this;

By the empty tracks I dozed among the wreckage
of my unfinished journey, drifted through flower-names,
the tall spiky plants that thrive on dry ground among ruins:

at dusk they look like ghosts, souls who dwell in fields
of—yes, *asphodel*. I'm haunted by the word, soft mantra
that belies the acid wasteland where it grows, wild, knavish,

derivation unknown. For comfort I try instead to dream
about the statue of the charioteer I'd seen at Delphi,
his onyx eyes and silver eyelashes, his damp side-curls,

the Ionic column of his pleated tunic that the violence
of the race can never perturb. He hovers serenely between
earth and heaven, lit from above; my ideal lover.

III.

And so, of course, to Apollo, whose torso still turns stone
to poetry, explodes the watching self from deep inside—
a starburst that's Greek for 'you have to change your life'; as if

I didn't know. To know and not to know, to be beside oneself,
to be out of one's mind, the Greeks had a word for this too.
Achilles, whose rage made the first word of the first poem.

IV.
Now look again at the bronze charioteer, his long toes
and the way the reins hang expertly in his elegant hands:
beauty to make anyone gasp. But the straightened back

and remote gaze give him away — he's a *kouros* in disguise,
archaic to his fingernails, behind that subtle brow
is the blackened shrunken leather of his real self's head.

Alien is the word I'm reaching for: the intake of breath,
because the past — which was known and could be recited[1] —
is suddenly unknown. Impossible to find a self-cure for this.

V.
We sit across the table from each other, a slight draught
from an open window stealing the heat out of the day.
What is there for us to talk about after all these years?

For the sake of something to say, I argue that Antigone
was wrong, that there's no catharsis if Kreon is only

---

1 Adam Phillips, *In Writing* (London: Hamish Hamilton, 2016).

and forever a tyrant, that tragedy is always a dilemma

of two impossible choices each with consequences
no-one save blind Tiresias can foresee. Should I say
that when I look at you these days I do not recognise

the man I loved immoderately, insanely as any Helen
or Ariadne? Should I wear my hair in snake-locks?
There are no stage directions in the tragic plays.

If knowledge is virtue, as the philosopher keeps telling us,
there's no excuse for doing bad; the greatest good
must be to *know thyself*. Last night I lay awake with rage:

I've forgotten why we came at all, the landscape's barren,
the smell of thyme illusory. We stare past each other
in the unsparing light, prattling in a dead language.

VI.
The afternoon slants across my book; it's autumn again
and I'm re-reading *The Greeks and the Irrational*, the chapter
about shame and guilt, how unconfessed desires and dreads

take shape as jealous gods. How deliverance does not come.
I fancy Picasso could have found his *demoiselles* in Hellas,
Klytemnestra's massive masked Erinyes sunning themselves

on the beach between sacrifices, unmoved by human reason.
Is it the playwright's sleight of hand that placates them,
the Kindly Ones, or does their change of heart conceal a
    truth?

VII.
I glance up and oh there you are, the light behind you,
and this time re-estranged as if you, or I, have been granted
an acquittal. I fold my body into yours as into darkness.

One Bright Day
Katharine Teleki

My father was a large-framed and booming man with a thick Hungarian accent. Imprinted on my mind are the childhood memories of him leaning in the doorway of our Houston, Texas home, aggravated by his family of women—me, my three older sisters, and my mom—taking forever to get out of the house. "Come on!" he would shout. "You are pissing away the day!"

He was born in 1929 in the Transylvania region of Hungary and grew up a privileged child. His father was a member of the nobility, a count by title, a charismatic, eccentric, multilingual aristocrat who had written a book on his agricultural innovations and wanted to have it translated into French. My grandmother was a rare independent female student from an intellectual family, who had studied at the Sorbonne in Paris and was bored by all her potential suitors. She agreed to work on the translation. Though he was much older and their subsequent relationship had many complications, they eventually married in 1928 and quickly had two boys, first my father and then my uncle.

By the time World War II approached, this marriage of two brilliant and strong-willed people was faltering—the primary conflict being how to school their boys. Then, while the family was separated in 1942, my grandfather unexpectedly died. In wartime, the noble title my grandmother took from

Analog Sea

Dear Reader,

So you managed to find us amid all the flickering and noise. Thank you for that, and for supporting your local bookstores and writers.

If you discover something valuable in this work, please tell other daydreamers about Analog Sea, our books, our biannual journal, *The Analog Sea Review,* and our wish for a little slowness now and then.

And if you want to stay in touch, to receive our seasonal bulletins and other mailings, why not send us a letter? Be sure to include your name, mailing address, and perhaps what was happening when you first discovered the Analog Sea.

Poems, drawings, and other outpourings of solitude are always welcome.

Yours truly,
Analog Sea

Basler Strasse 115
79115 Freiburg

PO Box 11670
Austin, TX 78711

her marriage became a major liability instead of a privilege. She vowed never to live behind the communist lines she saw coming, and in the winter of 1944–45 decided to flee west and seek a different path for her two boys, then aged twelve and fourteen.

They left with only winter clothes and food, and faced a harrowing escape to Switzerland across Hungary and Austria, often on foot. On their way, they sought out a school where my grandmother's sister had been head teacher, but they found it had been converted into a field hospital for the German army. That night, crammed alongside wounded soldiers in dank underground cellars, they heard a deafening crash followed by a series of thuds, and then silence. The next morning, the boys emerged from the cellar and saw fires burning, telephone wires down, the church on the square damaged by shrapnel. And then they saw the bomb that had gone through the building at a 45-degree angle. It had passed through the roof, three stories, and the side wall. Finally, it had landed on its side, unexploded, dug halfway into the lawn. My uncle remembers the exceptionally bright day and the green grass of the lawn. He remembers seeing the bomb lodged in the lawn and thinking, "That's why we are alive." He told me, "I felt somehow, I don't know, euphoric. I thought, 'I'm alive!' And by God, I was going to kick that bomb. 'I'm alive and you are dead. I will kick you!'" And my father pulled him back, saying, "Don't do that!"

My father never told us about this unexploded bomb, but he taught us about it in other, subtler ways. Every Thanksgiving for many years, he would drag us all to a mouse-infested cabin on a mountainous and remote Far West Texas cattle ranch. He would lecture us on many things, but not on this point; he just drove us the two days to get out there, woke us up for the sunrises, played cards with us for hours, and took us on impossible hikes up craggy mountains at very young ages. It was only recently when I traveled through the Carpathian Mountains where he grew up that I understood he was quietly trying to share the most joyous and peaceful moments of his youth with us, before his parents' separation, before the war.

Since my father's sudden death in 2013, I've come to realize that his endless aggravation at a sense of wasting time on meaningless things was a gift. For so much of my life, I dismissed his character as a collection of peculiar quirks. My heart aches now remembering all the times his frustrated refrain, "You're pissing away the day!" would fall on deaf ears in our loud, hectic house. In a culture filled with self-help books and a booming industry of "mindfulness" products, I think of my father and his drive to live a purposeful life. It seems the key truths to life are frustratingly simple; it's the honest day-to-day part that is hardest.

My mind returns again and again to the clarity of the blue sky and the green grass on a morning after a bombing raid, to the image of a teenage boy pulling his brother back. I keep a picture of my father and grandmother, later in their lives, on my desk. When I'm down in the weeds, pissing away my time, they help me lift my gaze to the horizon.

Interview with Godfrey Reggio
Richard Whittaker

O ne Friday morning I happened to tune in to KQED's morning program *Forum*, where an interview with Philip Glass and Godfrey Reggio was underway. They were in town for a weekend showing at Davies Symphony Hall of Reggio's *Qatsi* Trilogy: *Koyaanisqatsi*, *Powaqqatsi*, and *Naqoyqatsi*. Philip Glass and his ensemble would be performing the music he had composed for the films. *Koyaanisqatsi* left a deep impression on me when I first watched it in 1983, as did *Powaqqatsi*, which came out five years later.

I picked up the phone and called KQED. It was a long shot. Was there any way I could interview Reggio? Godfrey, it turned out, was willing to meet with me, though this would have to happen on the fly. That's how, the next day, I found myself sitting across from Reggio himself, an event I could not have imagined twenty-four hours earlier. After the interview, strolling together in friendly conversation, life could hardly have seemed better.

RICHARD WHITTAKER: I'm struck by your discovery of the importance of the things we do every day. Can you say more about that?

GODFREY REGGIO: I was in Albuquerque in the early 90s and the Dalai Lama was at the University of New Mexico giving a talk. The place was packed. A woman jumped up and asked, "Your Holiness, what is the single most important thing that I could give attention to?" Without even a thought, he answered, "routine." Now, I understood that immediately. In my order,[1] the rule, or routine, was the highest order of attention, that is, being attentive to what one did every day — because what we do is what we become. Although we consider our brain our largest organ, our minds are a deceptively small part of who we are.

RW: The attentiveness, that's the thing, right? Because my routine is usually just a place for daydreaming.

GR: Exactly. In Sanskrit there's a word, *ekagrata*, which means one-pointedness — the ability to focus on something. That ability to persistently focus is what gives one the ability to do things that are beyond our wildest imagination. But that's not something we learn. It's something we have to struggle to acquire. I look at it as commitment. Once you commit yourself, everything changes; everything comes to you. There's that great quote attributed to Goethe: "Whatever you can do, or think you can do, do it! Boldness has genius in it." We're capable, literally, of extraordinary things, being very ordinary people.

---

1 Congregatio Fratrum Christianorum, Congregation of Christian Brothers.

RW: Would you say something more about what might go along with what you've called "growing up in the Middle Ages."

GR: I'll use a reference to Joseph Brodsky, the expatriate from the old Soviet Union, an American poet laureate in 1991, I think. He begins *Less Than One*[2] with his explanation of Marx's great conundrum: is it your mind that determines your behavior or your behavior that determines your mind? Brodsky knew that for most people, our behavior determines the content of our mind, because we're creatures of habituation. His brilliant insight on how to change one's mind is to change one's behavior, and his response to that conundrum of Marx's was to step outside of the world and yet be in it. So I'm referring to the Middle Ages in that sense of being outside of contemporary American life.

RW: I was listening to a radio program where two philosophy professors were discussing the question, if technology produces pills that we can take which will make us happy and healthy, is there any reason not to use them? In other words, to rely on whatever new wonders technology comes up with "to help us"? I saw that something had already seeped into me.

2 Joseph Brodsky, *Less Than One: Selected Essays* (New York: Farrar, Straus and Giroux, 1986).

I had already been infiltrated, so to speak. I agree with your use of the word hubris to refer to our imagining that we are in control of these new powers.

GR: Well, following up on what you're saying, which I think I understand very well, I used myself as the subject for my films. All these things that I'm talking about I can see and feel in myself. I become the environment I'm brought up in and so I have the ability, as any human does, if I wish to, to reflect on my own condition. So I've been the basis of my films. I don't say that in any glorious way. I say it just to be honest. I'm basing it on my own experience of the world. I'm not saying it's the right experience, or that it's the truth, but I don't want to be offering the audience a fraud.

I know that film is so powerful that one can question the probity of free will in the presence of this electronic fire. We have the extraordinary examples of propaganda that came with the motion picture camera. The effect of propaganda on people is enormous. The very word "documentary" shares its etymology with the word "docile." And we are very docile beings. We're loaded with fragility. This is also our beauty, but we're highly suggestible, especially in the crowd, and we're sort of living in the crowd by virtue of the mass society that we're part of.

RW: I suspect you're not a big fan of advertising.

GR: No. I'm not. But I will give you an anecdote. Someone who was very significant in my starting all of this was Jerry Mander.[3] He wrote this incredible book *The Four Arguments for the Elimination of Television*.[4] He came out of an advertising background and started Public Media Center here in town. I came to seek him out before I did any films here in San Francisco. And with Ron Fricke, my colleague on *Koyaanisqatsi*, I did a multimedia saturation campaign using television, billboards, radio, newspapers, and lectures for one month. I wanted to use advertisement because people are irrevocably hooked to it. You can't escape it. It's like the wallpaper we live in. I wanted to take something and advertise nothing, have no tags on it. They told me you can't advertise something without a tag on it. It's against FCC regulations. So I made tags so small that they couldn't be seen.

RW: One of the things that's occurred to me with regard to language has to do with the word *being*. It's not a word we talk about and not something at all accessible to the world of science. If you were to look closely enough, it must be that everyone has this experience of being here in the world which we have poor language for but which is felt as the mystery and

---

3 Jerry Mander is an activist and author born in 1936, raised in New York, and presently living in California.

4 Jerry Mander, *The Four Arguments for the Elimination of Television* (New York: William Morrow, 1978).

wonder of life. And we don't have a culture that recognizes this or supports it. So it gets lost and people have to make a living. They fall under the mass ways of living and forget.

GR: Yes, because nobody teaches you to be an individual. Education could be much more dynamic and interesting. It should be something where people could create things that have never been seen or heard before. We're here as creators. We're really toolmakers, *Homo faber*, as well as *Homo sapiens*. We become what we do.

A Sunset and a Cone
William Oxley

The sea soaps up the weathered shore
below pines like tall men, luminous
in an incredible sunset there.

Startled I pick up a fallen cone—
old wood among green needles—
that is life dead and gone

though old wives and children say
from its spent pores you can tell the weather
an open and shut case of prophecy.

It is then I realize not the need
for God, but the huge gulf the senses create
that cannot be otherwise filled,

for beauty is so ordinary, so everywhere—
the beginning, middle and end of all light—
something that can bruise and brighten

leaving us weeping and loving
before the anonymity of
a blown cone, a day's cosmetic dying.

Metaphora
Robert Ensor

Guarding the illustrious, eloquent garden
Is Metaphora, a female owl with maternal face
And eyes the size of shattered saucers:
One resembles an ancient
Rheumy sun, and one fierce
As a recent moon born out of wedlock.

The old eye watches out for the elderly,
The infirm and those who believe in dreams
Whilst the new eye chases baby mice,
Children who play truant and brooks babbling
In foreign tongues and telling watery tales.

This is not a perfect situation for eyes that mesmerize.
But even a broken clock tells
The correct time at least twice a day.

Music, a Life-Changing Force
Jameela Siddiqi

My first experience of Indian classical music turned my life inside-out and upside-down. While most of us can narrate an incident related to our particular kind of music and our life's personal soundtrack, I believe Indian classical music is the most potent in terms of transforming lives. To paraphrase the great Sufi teacher, Hazrat Inayat Khan, it is that endless ocean into which one goes on diving to find more pearls. Yehudi Menuhin described his first experience of Indian music as "being carried away with wonderment." That was in the 1930s but he could have been describing my first encounter with Indian music, some fifty years later, in 1989, when I attended a private recital—held in a small art gallery in West London—by someone I had never heard of.

I sat cross-legged on the floor, just a few feet away from one of the greatest musicians the world has known: the late Sufi singer Nusrat Fateh Ali Khan. I was really only there for an evening out but once Khan started singing it felt to me as though all the secrets of the universe were being unveiled one by one, bringing a deep sense of peace and fulfillment.

It wasn't as though I hadn't heard or admired music before that evening. Like all my peers in the cultural hybridity that prevailed in what used to be British Colonial East Africa, our Scottish music teacher in primary school had drilled me through all the verses of "Loch Lomond." I liked Elvis Presley and, in later years, Leonard Cohen. But I was equally enchanted with whatever I'd heard of Beethoven and Bach. Alongside The Beatles, I was also drawn to the protest music of that time, notably that of Bob Dylan. But Indian film music had always remained a favorite and, for many of us, also served as a rudimentary introduction to classical music. Indian film music was the original fusion music — long before the term had been coined — drawing as much from Indian classical music as it did from Mozart and Chopin. But nothing of this eclectic musical past had prepared me for what I was to hear that evening.

To give you some context, Indian classical music evolved from devotional rituals. It is one of the world's oldest music systems which is practiced, to this day, with many of its original rules intact. Those rules, in turn, have led to an entire etiquette that is now deeply embedded within the music and its delivery. Not only do they apply to performing musicians and what they may, or may not, do but equally stringent rules of conduct also apply to listeners. While musicians are bound by far-reaching requirements such as the water-tight grammar of *ragas*, or musical scales for melodic improvisation, down to the minutest detail such as how wide singers are permitted to open their mouths, the audience, for their part, are prescribed the correct way of sitting at a recital. They must resist the desire to appear to, or to literally, nod off and must never point their feet at the musician or the musical instruments.

Of course, some of these rules are impossible to enforce in Western-style concert halls where, at least on one occasion, a senior Indian maestro has had to gently admonish a courting couple seated in the front row.

The etiquette of Indian classical music has been handed down to us from an era when the only way to listen was by sitting cross-legged on the floor, at the same level as the performer. Only in that position could you be sure that every single sound vibration was felt while also maintaining eye contact with the musician. Eye contact was vital and required a brightly-lit room. The semi-darkness and hushed tranquility of a Western concert hall is alien to this tradition. Modern concert hall architecture has forced some flexibility in seating positions but it's not unknown for Indian musicians, even today at venues such as the Barbican or the Royal Festival Hall in London, to request that the auditorium lights be left on since being able to see the audience is an essential part of their music. Applause is considered extremely vulgar but, at an appropriate point, an audible verbal exclamation of praise—not for the musician but for God—is almost mandatory.

Despite this need for constant interaction, the entire Indian classical music system is based on restraint. Musicians are required to exercise the utmost restraint and avoid drawing attention to themselves or their musical wizardry. Instead, they should act only as a medium through whom a *raga* unfolds in a way that suggests it is newly discovered. The listener, too, is required to receive the music as though it were being heard for the very first time.

Ancient treatises on Indian music speak of two kinds of sound: that which is struck—and heard—and that which is unstruck but felt rather than heard. It is this unstruck sound— the ever-present celestial music—which human beings are said to crave and, on feeling it, the soul is said to feel liberated. It is asserted that every single stimulant or mind-altering substance that has been sought by mankind has been a futile attempt to try to capture something of this eternal sound, but has only resulted in a pale and short-lived imitation of the real thing. Music—and music alone—has the power to lead us to the ultimate sound of the spheres.

Indian classical music does not seek to create a mood but rather to explore that mood, examining it from every angle and plumbing its very depths. A core belief is that which remains unsaid is more enticing and indescribably more meaningful than that which is explicitly stated. It is this belief that makes the spaces between the musical notes—the sounds that are felt rather than heard—the essential element of this music. For discerning listeners, the presence of microtones—or *shruti*, as they are known—is often the main factor in distinguishing a good musical performance from an outstanding one.

The etiquette of listening to Indian classical music is not only consistent with its devotional roots that lie in the chanting of the sacred verses that the Aryans brought to India thousands of years ago, but is also in line with courtly manners. Those manners evolved over hundreds of years as the music was developing into the artful music performed at India's many royal courts, or Darbars. As this process went on, gestures began to take the place of words as needless verbosity is considered superfluous in a space which is soon to be filled with music. A slight raising of the hand, or a discreet nod at an accompanying musician or even the humility with which a classical maestro requests the permission of the senior-most listener in order to begin a performance—these are remnants from the golden age of courtly music. And, even more antiquated than that, the respect and reverence for age and musical virtuosity—often enacted by bending to touch the feet of maestros and musical gurus, coupled with an involuntary tug of the ear which signifies an act of repentance when daring to mention the name of a distinguished musical figure—are all part of this coded language and have reached us more or less as laid down in ancient times.

Ancient though it may be, for me Indian classical music was born on a cold December evening in 1989 in that small space of a West London art gallery where some eighty of us, unbothered by the pins and needles in our feet, sat huddled together on the floor, transfixed by Nusrat Fateh Ali Khan.

Khan was a performer of *qawwali*, the music of South Asian Sufis, or Islamic mystics. A thirteenth-century off-shoot of Indian classical music, it is performed at the tombs of great Sufi masters of the past. Qawwali consists of verses drawn from the poetry of Muslim as well as Hindu and Sikh mystic poets which are sung within the confines of Indian *ragas* and laced with hypnotic, trance-inducing rhythms. In its essence it is music with a message: peace, love, and a celebration of the unity of mankind. That it is able to have such a tremendous impact even when there isn't a Sufi tomb anywhere in sight, is a tribute to its timeless, all-embracing expression of love.

At this point in my life I had spent nearly two decades working in television news with its daily offerings of mostly man-made atrocities. The question that was paramount in my mind that evening, was this: When human beings are capable of so much love and the ability to convey it with such beauty, why then do they focus, mostly, on causing untold misery for their fellow-humans? I myself felt jarred by the banality of what I had thought constituted fulfillment, that is to say the sense of bloated pride which came from beating the opposition to a breaking news story.

So, what happened to me that night? If I could capture it in mere words, I would be exceptionally gifted but, with hindsight, I can only venture to guess that Khan's music raised me to a higher level of consciousness. I was reminded of a favorite childhood story, that of the Hindu god Krishna who played his bamboo flute somewhere in the forest. In the dead of night, the pretty milkmaids of the region would leave their beds—and their husbands—compelled to follow the sound of Krishna's flute deep into the forest.

This was the evening I had finally heard the sound of Krishna's flute, not played by a Hindu god but by a Muslim Sufi musician. The experience was overwhelming. Drawn as Krishna's milkmaids, I found that I could not turn back. I made what appeared to be a rash and, what seems even now, a rather astonishing decision. I was going to walk away from television news and all its little glories and go after this music.

Apart from just having realized that the longest distance in the world was probably the distance between two musical notes, I had no training whatsoever. The whole of the Indian classical system—and this particular brand of Sufi music that had emerged from it—seemed like a highly sophisticated code, just waiting to be deciphered. And yet, in some mysterious way, I had been given instant access. Where career, ambition, and personal progress had appeared to be clear and well-signposted, the way ahead, squeezed as it were between the minutest microtone of two notes, now beckoned. I was embarking on what was to be nearly three decades of decoding this music for its many thousands of enthusiasts and, if I could, for those yet to discover it.

The Sufi message of peace and love in Khan's music seemed to point the way to an ideal existence which could end all human misery. Yet, in that same year (1989) when the message of the Islamic mystics had led to my personal renaissance, the world had seen a very different version of Islam. An Ayatollah in Iran passed a fatwa calling for the murder of British writer Salman Rushdie—and this at a time when heaving concert halls from Tokyo to Berlin and Sydney to New York were swaying to the message of mystical Islam, as brought to them by Nusrat Fateh Ali Khan.

Khan sang in a number of languages including Persian, Hindi, Urdu and Punjabi but the vast majority of his audiences did not understand any of them. Indian as well as Chinese sages have pointed to the main difference between the two principal components of music, stating that while rhythm appeals to the more animalistic part of human nature, causing a direct physical response in the body—hence martial music to help soldiers march more willingly towards death or glory—melody is more attractive to highly evolved souls.

So could it be that Khan's vast international audiences were reacting only to the pounding, pulsating rhythms of *qawwali* music and that its essential message of peace and unity was being completely bypassed? I put this question to Khan himself, when I had the good fortune of interviewing him shortly before his death in 1997. He was of the view that music by itself was sufficient to carry the Sufi message and language was not a barrier, adding that although the majority may get carried away by those intoxicating rhythms, even if one person in a thousand felt his "heart turning," the job of a Sufi musician was done.

At that point in the interview, we both fell silent. Given that those mystical places between sounds remain more beautiful when unstated, I like to think I exercised the utmost restraint in not blurting out that his music may, very well, have turned my heart.

Program Notes
Ravi Shankar In Concert

Tuesday Folk Club

The system of Indian music is known as *raga sangeet*, which can be traced back nearly two thousand years. A *raga* is difficult to explain to a Western listener because it is neither a scale nor a mode. It is, however, a scientific, precise, subtle, and aesthetic melodic form with its own peculiar ascending and descending movement, which consists of either a full octave or a series of six or five notes.

Several characteristics can differentiate one *raga* from another: the subtle difference in the order of notes, an omission of one or more jarring or dissonant notes, an emphasis on a particular note, the slide from one note to another, and the use of microtones, along with other subtleties.

There are seventy-two *mela*, or parent scales, on which *ragas* are based. Each *raga* has its own principal mood—such as tranquility, devotion, eroticism, loneliness, pathos, heroism, etc.—and is associated, according to its mood, with a particular time of the day or night and a season.

Between twenty-five and ninety percent of Indian music is improvisation depending upon the imagination and creativity of an artist, and a great artist is able to deliver and instill in the listener the mood of the *raga* being played.

Analog Sea Editor's Note

THIS TEXT WAS TAKEN FROM a stray concert program from a Ravi Shankar concert held at a certain Tuesday Folk Club, location unknown, circa 1964. The program was discovered serendipitously in an old vinyl record acquired in a used record store. Not knowing where the event was held gives it a special significance, underlining the ephemeral quality of live performance before the age of incessant documentation.

Shankar writes of a saying in Sanskrit—*ranjayathi iti ragah*—"that which colors the mind is a *raga*." He explains, "For a *raga* to truly color the mind of the listener, its effect must be created not only through the notes and the embellishments but also by the presentation of the specific emotion or mood characteristic of each *raga*. Thus through rich melodies in our music, every human emotion, every subtle feeling in man and nature can be musically expressed and experienced."

Interview with Jameela Siddiqi
Analog Sea Editors

Analog Sea editors, Jonathan Simons and Janos Tedeschi had the pleasure recently of sharing tea and words with writer and novelist, Jameela Siddiqi.

ANALOG SEA: You've spoken about first discovering classical Indian music in the late 1980s and how you would travel great distances to attend live performances. Does technology now make it easier to access great music? Has it become too easy?

JAMEELA SIDDIQI: It has and it hasn't. It's easier in the sense of accessing information—data—via the Internet. But the Internet isn't going to tell you, "This guy's good." It's not going to tell you, "This person has severely abbreviated the music in order to get maximum concert bookings and corporate sponsorship."

AS: And now we can pipe in entertainment at all hours. I wonder whether live performance was more special when the home wasn't so connected. As a young adult, for better or worse, did you have time when you were in silence or solitude?

JS: Yes, more solitude than I wanted at that age but I never saw it as solitude because I was young and stupid. I saw it as loneliness. Now I crave for solitude. But before, it was more about how on Monday I was already thinking, "What am I doing this weekend? I don't want to be in on a Saturday night." But after that I kept feeling the need to be by myself. I wanted to be alone just to have enough space around me. I liked just sitting. Sometimes I would listen to music and sometimes I wouldn't. Even thirty minutes of quiet would rejuvenate me.

But in today's culture—like the L'Oréal ads, they do this "I'm worth it" number and call solitude "me time." But it wasn't *me time*. It was about just wanting to sit quietly. I still like sitting quietly. And when thoughts come, you just observe them as they go by. It regularizes the breathing, evens the blood pressure.

AS: If one never has that space in solitude or stillness, if you're constantly distracted by notifications on your telephone or by the next thing that says, "I'm important," there will never be a moment for one to connect on a vertical axis.

JS: That nags at me all the time, that constant interacting with the world. But then, the sages say, "It's all too easy. You want to go and sit on a mountaintop in the Himalayas. That's great, but that's not a challenge. The challenge is to live in this world but free of it."

AS: When I was a touring musician on the concert stage, before the days of ubiquitous Internet, I was always the most interesting thing happening in the hall. Now the most interesting thing is the audience member's smartphone. It connects him or her to everyone they love and everything that interests them. To sing a sad song, a ballad, forget it!

JS: But why is that? Is that because people have lost the capacity for emotionalizing that sadness? Or is it because they're no longer sad? That can't be true.

AS: Maybe the space is uncomfortable and now there's something that offers us the possibility to stay in a perpetual state of comfort; that's what the smartphone does. Back when boredom was inescapable—sitting on the train, waiting for a bus—you could sit just staring at a tree or observing your breath, or you could feel sad, or you could feel all sorts of things.

They have a word in Silicon Valley for this; it's called *friction*. It's the discomfort that a person feels waiting in line or at a concert when the song gets a little slow. The goal, and the capitalistic drive behind all of these applications and gadgets, is to eliminate friction. Of course, psychic discomfort is friction, as is boredom. Ultimately, sickness and death are also friction. They're working on that, too.

JS: Oh yeah, death is particularly embarrassing. The only certainty we have in life is the one that's not allowed to be discussed.

AS: I'm interested in how all this impacts the creative process, and particularly your writing.

JS: I write offline. I cannot have messages or notifications intruding. It's too distracting. The funny thing is, I knew I'd married the right man because he was the first person who could be the other person in the room and I could still write. Whereas normally I couldn't. If I had a friend nearby and they said, "No, carry on, do your work, I'll just read the paper," I couldn't write. But somehow with my husband, I feel that he melts into the background. That's my yardstick for knowing if it's right or wrong.

AS: Do you struggle with writing? How do you approach a difficult period?

JS: Whatever chapter's not working, whatever paragraph I'm not happy with—I always leave it to bake until the next day. This gives me a chance to clear out some of the mess. I start at a certain hour, because the brain can be trained to yield at a particular time. Even when I work alone, I never work in a dressing gown. You work fully dressed, with makeup if possible, like you would at the office. You sit at a computer dressed, you work, stop for lunch, don't answer calls except in your break. I don't go into the kitchen until I log off the computer at six thirty.

AS: We've spoken previously about art being political. After the Second World War, a common sentiment being written in the papers by artists and poets was, "There's nothing we can say now. What can we possibly say?" They seem to have been suggesting that beyond journalism and dealing with the facts, there's no place for art and poetry in such a horrific moment in history. What do you think of this in the current context?

JS: Well, art and poetry born out of pain or oppression, if that's all that's behind it, is extremely sad. So much of what the Allies were putting out was pure propaganda. I don't think the real artists were allowed to express what they were really feeling because that's the nature of war. Each side has to spew propaganda. You have falsifications, we force our artists to express them, and at the end of it, win or lose, your artists are absolutely drained. If they've allowed themselves to be controlled by the war propaganda, what are they going to do for real when the war's over?

AS: Everyone has to choose sides.

JS: I hear cartoonists these days saying, "The news is so ridiculous we couldn't make it up. We do satire but now the news itself is satire." Art has got to be more than that. Art isn't just about satirizing society or politics. I believe art is about pain. The person who satirizes the situation laughs, because otherwise they'd cry, wouldn't they?

AS: So is it about overcoming one's own pain? And in such times, does it become an obligation for the artist or writer to create?

JS: Regardless of whether anyone's going to read or not, you have to write. If I have a problem, any kind of problem, I'll write it down. Then it jumps out at me, the options and possible solutions. Unless I see it written, I cannot even see the whole problem clearly. It's in the writing that the problems reveal themselves. Unless I see it written, it almost doesn't exist for me. It's weird, isn't it?

AS: Pen and paper.

JS: I went to school in the good days in a British colony, where you were given new writing supplies at the start of every term. And today, when I go to Ryman Stationery, if

I've got my credit card on me, it's like the end of the world. I still like buying notebooks. I have notebooks everywhere for every project I'm working on. It's the medium. The act of writing actually reinforces memory. The writer connects it to the memory. V.S. Naipaul never typed. He scribbled the most atrocious-looking scratchings and then went to a paid typist. He's a hell of a writer, but he could not write unless he wrote by hand.

AS: Nietzsche said that when he started typing on a typewriter it changed his way of thinking entirely. The medium keeps getting faster which means less time walking to the post office or filling up a fountain pen. That "accidental time" is incredibly important for thinking, for brainstorming. This is why I like a certain amount of old technology in my daily routine because it forces me to slow down.

JS: I still send birthday cards in the post because I like choosing them. I like the opportunity to go into the paper store and look at all the cards. I like the artwork. It's a real treat. And people say, "Oh, it's just a waste. They get binned. Why don't you send an e-card?" I like writing personal messages. I was thrilled to get your [Analog Sea] letter in the mail. I didn't keep my typewriter but I do handwrite notes. So it's about reconnecting to the way we were and keeping that avenue open where we did certain things a particular way that kept our consciousness in a particular frame of mind.

AS: Definitely.

JS: It's got nothing to do with divorcing from reality; that's actually how we lived one-hundred percent of the time before now. Whenever I do log off, I feel a strange kind of intrusion has gone away.

AS: We're living in a very strange time. You talked earlier about the possible disintegration of the European Union. In America, we have a television president. So where does it end?

JS: A child with his finger on the nuclear codes.

AS: But where is the writer in all of this? Where is the novelist and the artist? Where is the musician? Those of us who can dream, where is the dreamer in all of this?

JS: I dream, therefore I am. That's my mantra. You have to live in the world, but live on some other planet at the same time. Just tell yourself you are from somewhere else and had to make a crash-landing here for some emergency; but you're not really from here. That's how I survive.

AS: Be in the world but not of it. But what's the work? What's the work of the dreamer, having crash-landed into this strange place?

JS: I think what binds us—regardless of the world situation—is pain, because we've all experienced it. What you or I call pain is the same but what pains us is completely different. And this is where I think art comes in, because the purpose of art is to artfully deal with that pain and explain it eloquently enough so that another person who has had that experience can stand aside from it and say, "Yes, I know what that feels like." It has to come from something much more universal.

When you think about it, everything changes—technology and everything else we're talking about. But the basic human emotions are there. Feelings have changed, yes. There's very little boredom now and people aren't as engaged in what they do. Nothing is internalized the way it used to be, but joy, sorrow, anger, jealousy, wonderment, they are all absolutely there. Nothing changes that. When we stop feeling those things, I think that is when we've really got trouble.

AS: You say, "When we stop feeling." Have we not already stopped feeling on some level?

JS: No. People are still getting jealous, they're still getting angry. They're still falling in love. They're still struck with wonderment. Might be at the wrong things. They might look at a skyscraper in Dubai and go "wow," but at least that feeling of *wow* is still there. But I don't think those emotions have gone away.

AS: Would you agree that the most rebellious thing a person might do now is to log offline, even temporarily?

JS: Hmm. Yes.

AS: I mean, isn't that an act of rebellion at this point?

JS: Yes, it is. We have to be very clear about the things that are possible today that weren't possible thirty years ago, things that help us to connect. But I think the speed is the main difference — the instantaneousness we expect in everything now.

But yes, being offline would be one of the most radical things to do. But even more radical, I go for long walks without my phone. When I go out and haven't got a phone, I have a word for that feeling: I feel *unanchored*.

AS: I think freedom would also be a word we could use. Could you tell us about a time recently when you felt free?

JS: I stood in the slave chamber in Zanzibar in November. I wasn't going to go, but my brother texted me from London and said, "Now come on, your niece and nephew need to see this. Don't suppress this. Go!" I was dreading it because that was the main holding port for slaves. God, I stood in that chamber and just cried. There was nothing I could do. I just cried. Because my imagination takes me to fifty men in this room, in this space, the tree where they were whipped. I only did it because my brother said, "Don't be a coward. Go in, take pictures, show them to your niece and nephew. They're learning about slavery." It was so painful.

AS: Perhaps it helps to accept the fact that we human beings are well-dressed monkeys with this unfortunate proclivity towards war and greed, the whole gamut. Then when there's beauty or the opportunity to have a little leisure to create beauty, to write a story and these kinds of things, then it's like, "Wow, that's really precious."

JS: Artists must suffer perpetually as a result of what's around them, the injustice against which they feel helpless. And don't you ever wonder how that beauty takes shape? Could it have come out of confronting something very ugly or having those thoughts yourself and then transforming them?

AS: For us, Analog Sea is really a quiet little song, a little songbird singing out into nothingness. But it is a product of several years of being quite frustrated by how things are evolving and wanting to do something transformative, like a little songbird sitting on a branch, creating a little bit of beauty.

JS: Well, I really like that idea. I find it very exciting.

The Old Poets
Jonathan Simons

The old poets
spent their summers
inscribing hidden words
into the trunks of ancient trees.

You can find their poems still,
and their diagrams,
and their invisible tracks
leading you deeper into the wood.

The old poets
spent winter
by candle flame, alone
translating nature,
a sort of levitation,
watching snow fall.

Loneliness and History
Leonard Cohen

In late December 1964, Canadian poet, writer, and singer-songwriter Leonard Cohen delivered a speech at the Jewish Public Library in Montreal. By this time, Cohen was already a known figure in his native country, a leading poet who captured the zeitgeist with a wit and irreverence that belied the profound subjects he explored. Today, going on six years since Cohen's death, all that survives of this remarkable speech are the following notes salvaged from his personal journal.

I am afraid I am going to talk about myself. All of my best friends are Jews but I am the only Jew I know really well. I have lived outside of any strong community and know nothing about the Talmud. I have no statistics on the community. It will survive, I hope, but I dare not speak of survival. There are too many big numbers in the air; too much sad confetti falls from the trains.

In Montreal we have always thought of ourselves as a community in the American sense, and our problems were about preserving our identity within the melting pot. We might find ourselves a minority but not in a melting-pot situation but rather in a very European situation. Again we will be Jews in the midst of a homogeneous nation with their own national culture and religion—a European predicament which I believe we are not at all prepared to encounter.

The only thing I can do, indeed must do, is make some kind of personal statement. I do not regard a speech before people as a casual luxury; that is why I prefer to read poems which I have worked on. I do not like to waste collective time. So I have tried to prepare a personal statement for tonight. It deals with ideas which are of great concern to me at the moment.

I remember A.M. Klein[1] speaking—A.M. Klein, whose poems disturbed me because at certain crucial moments he used the word "we" instead of "I" and because he spoke with too much responsibility; he was too much a champion of the cause, too much the theorist of the Jewish party line. But when he is true to his terror, then he sings; when he begs God to keep "the golden dome" of his mind safe from disease, offering as sacrificial payment his limbs, his body's health— then he sings out of the terror which makes a man lonely. Sometimes his nostalgia for a warm rich past becomes more than nostalgia—becomes, rather, an impossible longing, an absolute and ruthless longing for the presence of the divine, for the evidence of holiness. Then he is alone and I believe him. Then there is no room for "we" and if I want to join him I must make my own loneliness.

But he has fallen into silence, and the silence is a warning. Klein is the last Jewish writer whom the rabbis and

---

1 Abraham Moses Klein (1909–1972) was a Ukrainian-born Canadian writer and lawyer who lived most of his life in Montreal.

businessmen will love. His silence marks the beginning of a massive assault, a literary assault, on this community. Klein chose to be a priest though it was a prophet we needed. He watched honor migrate from the scholar to the manufacturer where it hardened into arrogant self-defense. Bronze plaques bearing names like Bronfman and Beutel were fastened to modern buildings, replacing humbler buildings established by men who loved books.

There is only one emotion which money has ever extended to idealism—contempt. Very early in my life I met men who suffered under this contempt. They were the teachers in the Hebrew school I attended. I am just beginning to understand why we never took them seriously, why their authority was so easily undermined. It was because our parents held them in contempt. Because they were poor, because they were refugees, because they brought a broken, failed European past into this expensive synagogue, and because they were *shlemiels*[2]—that is, scholars. They smelled of failure, and how shabby they seemed beside the glittering seat-owner.[3] If ever a community succeeded in demonstrating its chosen values to its young, it was this community in its opposition of wealth and humiliation. The whole learning apparatus was on the level

---

2 From Yiddish שלימיל (*shlimil*) meaning bungler or fool.

3 Cohen refers to the practice, in some large synagogues in wealthier communities, of "buying" a prestigious, ornate, or front-row seat in the sanctuary through a large donation to the synagogue.

of a charity function. Teachers wore the bitter, obsequious expression of men on welfare, (and I say in parenthesis that we loved the one or two who dared to beat us) and our whole attendance had the atmosphere of an obligatory donation to the USA.

I will admit that the situation then was exaggerated because my synagogue was very rich, and more than one of its members had his fortune peddling the Talmud.

Klein saw this condition in communities across the country, but the Jews were under siege, so he became their clown. He spoke to men who despised the activity he loved most. He raised money. He chose to be a priest and to protect the dead rituals. And now we have his silence.

I do not think that any other writers from this community will make his mistake. They prefer the dialogue of exile, a dialogue which seems to be very one-sided, but it is still the old rich dialogue between the prophet and the priest.

I believe that at the beginning of an idea, each of the men who hold it is both a prophet and a priest. But as the energy of the idea diminishes, the functions of priest and prophet begin to split apart; soon, no single person can perform both offices. As the idea exhausts itself in failure, on absorption and dissipation into the masses, in combat with competing ideas, the function of the prophet becomes irreconcilable to the function of the priest.

The priest is the archetype of the community which the original idea called into being. The community is marked with fossils of the original energy and convinced that only adherence to the original forms can rejuvenate it. The community is like an old lady whose canary has escaped in a storm but who continues to furnish the cage with food and water and trapezes in the hope that the canary will come back. The priest tries to persuade her that this optimism is religion.

The prophet, on the other hand, continues to serve the idea even as it changes forms, trying never to mistake the cast-off shell with the swift-changing thing that shed it. He follows it into regions of danger so that he becomes alone, and by his nature becomes unwelcome to the community. The community is a museum of the old forms and dedicated to them. It changes very slowly and usually only under violence.

Some moment in time, there must very briefly have been among the ancient Hebrews men who were both prophet and priest in the same office. I tease my imagination when I try to conceive of the energy of that combination. Their lives burned with such an intensity that we can still feel the warmth. I love the Bible because it honors them.

By the time this idea seized Moses it was no longer young, and he needed to create and elaborate laws to bind himself to the community—for he was a prophet and he must have been anguished by the distance growing between himself and the community. When he smashed the tablets he signaled to all who followed him the futility of his project.

I do not know what that original idea was, that path which through the generations was attended with such beauty and terror — though I want to know. On those rare occasions when I purify myself I have an intimation.

I have tried to offer a definition of history. Now I shall try to define idea. Idea is the tongue of creation. It is the noise creation makes. Just as history is the biography of idea, idea is the birth notice and obituary of creation.

Well, you see how I have failed in my definition. All I know is that some men have drawn close to it, and have lived in its fire, and they are burning still. I believe they beheld a unity, a barbarous finality, a vision of completion which their individual personalities could not resist and so they surrendered them. They became the idea, or as the Christians say, the word became flesh. Thus they ventured into loneliness. Owning nothing, they would witness the divinity of everything. I know very little about this. I have tried to discipline myself, to prepare myself, but I've only gone so far as arrogance and attitude, which is not nutritious.

I believe the idea concerned the sense of universal holiness, of the incorruptibility of creation. Whatever it was, we still feel its power and we have a very particular treatment for those men who today move toward the idea. We force them into solitude or we exile or kill them. In my arrogance I wish to move among their huge shadows, rather than among the blinding shadows of the community.

I do not believe this philosophy has much of a chance. I think we have eliminated all but the most poisoned blasphemous ideas of God. I believe that the God in our synagogues is a hideous distortion of a supreme idea and deserves to be attacked and destroyed. I consider it my duty to expose the platitude which we have created.

Sunflowers
Richard Ormrod

For Vincent, sunflowers were emblematic
of vitality, light and life: ten
versions painted in as many years,
along with landscapes, walls, chairs,
so much *yellow*—
        to counteract
the inner dark that drove him on, revealed
Rembrandt-like in *The Potato Eaters*,
but most in self-immolation: bouts
of black misery, asperity and absinthe,
abject poverty, failed love-affaires …

Yet, in the Yellow House at Arles—shared
briefly with Gaugin—he began a manic
marathon: four paintings a week, minimum,
—one a day sometimes—pinning them
round the small, misshapen rooms
smelling of turps and tobacco …

Later, in the Asylum Garden
while others ranted or shouted
Vincent simply painted:
olive groves, white orchards, mid-
blue irises, yellow ground, red

dots and blotches in *Field with Poppies*
seen from his barred window...

His last whole year spent there
fighting hallucinations and despair, till
leaving its grim safety he fled where
birds gathered ominously overhead
hovering for their prey, as shown
on his last canvas, *Wheatfield with Crows*...
Nine weeks later he shot himself dead.

Theo, ever the protector-provider,
in a last, fitting, non-ironic gesture
put sunflowers on his grave.

I Never Wanted Fame
Antonio Machado

I have never wanted fame,
nor wanted to leave my poems
behind in the memory of men.
I love the subtle worlds,
delicate, almost without weight,
like soap bubbles.
I enjoy seeing them take color
of sunlight and scarlet, float
in the blue sky, then
suddenly quiver and break.

Antonio Machado, *I Never Wanted Fame,* trans. Robert Bly (St. Paul, Minnesota: Ally Press, 1979), p. 1.

When Death Comes
Mary Oliver

When death comes
like the hungry bear in autumn;
when death comes and takes all the bright coins
   from his purse

to buy me, and snaps the purse shut;
when death comes
like the measle-pox;

when death comes
like an iceberg between the shoulder blades,

I want to step through the door full of curiosity,
   wondering:
what is it going to be like, that cottage of darkness?

And therefore I look upon everything
as a brotherhood and a sisterhood,
and I look upon time as no more than an idea,
and I consider eternity as another possibility,

and I think of each life as a flower, as common
as a field daisy, and as singular,

and each name a comfortable music in the mouth,
tending, as all music does, toward silence,

and each body a lion of courage, and something
precious to the earth.

When it's over, I want to say: all my life
I was a bride married to amazement.
I was the bridegroom, taking the world into my arms.

When it's over, I don't want to wonder
if I have made of my life something particular, and real.
I don't want to find myself sighing and frightened,
or full of argument.

I don't want to end up simply having visited this world.

Artwork Credits

In order of appearance:

Joseph-Antoine d'Ornano
Unnamed, Cover Artwork, 2018
Watercolor

Kelley Van Dilla
無名の門 (*Unnamed Entrance*), 2018
Watercolor

Daniel Bodner
Beech Forest 1 (Study 2), 2012
Oil on linen

Manfred Kastner
Am Kai (At the pier)
Lithography
Courtesy of Sylvia Kastner and Dr. Willem Schoeber

Daniel Bodner
Beech Forest 2 (Study 2), 2011
Oil on linen

Contributors

EDITORS

Jonathan Simons, Analog Sea's founding editor, is an American writer living in Germany.

Janos Tedeschi is a Swiss-Italian filmmaker and artist.

Elena Fritz is a German editor and translator.

WRITERS

Leonard Cohen (1934–2016) was a Canadian singer-songwriter and writer.

Steven Doloff is a writer based in New York City.

Nathaniel Dorsky is an American experimental filmmaker.

Ralph Waldo Emerson (1803–1882) was an American essayist and poet.

Robert Ensor is a poet living between Spain and Ireland.

Matthew Feeney is a writer and former actor currently incarcerated in Minnesota.

E.M. Forster (1879–1970) was an English essayist and novelist.

Martha Graham (1894–1991) was an American dancer and choreographer.

Urs Hafner is a freelance historian and journalist based in Bern.

Byung-Chul Han is a South Korean-born German author and philosopher based in Berlin.

Matthew Hollis is an editor and poet living in London.

Trebbe Johnson is an author and activist who lives in rural Pennsylvania.

Kyra Levine is a writer, editor, and educator living in Europe and the United States.

Antonio Machado (1875–1939) was a Spanish poet from Seville.

Thomas Merton (1915–1968) was an American Trappist monk, activist, and writer.

Mary Oliver (1935–2019) was an American poet and essayist.

Richard Ormrod is a biographer, journalist, and poet who lives in Sussex, England.

William Oxley (1939–2020) was a British poet.

Carl Sagan (1934–1996) was an American astronomer and author.

Lesley Saunders, author of several books of poetry, lives in the United Kingdom.

Patrick Shen is a filmmaker living in
Los Angeles.

Jameela Siddiqi is a novelist and
journalist living in London.

Scott T. Starbuck is a poet living in
California and Washington.

Dr. James Suzman is an
anthropologist and author based
in the United Kingdom.

Katharine Teleki is a writer living in
Austin, Texas.

Richard Whittaker is a writer and
editor living in Berkeley, California.

ARTISTS

Daniel Bodner is an American
painter dividing his time between
Amsterdam, New York, and
Easthampton, Massachusetts.

Kelley Van Dilla is an American
director, actor, and visual artist.

Manfred Kastner (1943–1988) was a
painter and sculptor from the German
Democratic Republic.

Joseph-Antoine d'Ornano is a Parisian
painter and writer.